Grace: A STORY

GRACE
A STORY

Paul Davies

ECW PRESS

CANADIAN CATALOGUING IN PUBLICATION DATA

Davies, Paul, 1954–

Grace

ISBN 1-55022-275-9

I. Title.

PS8557.A8197G7 1996   C813'.54   C95-933133-6
PR9199.3.D38G7 1996

The cover image is a detail of 'Apollo and Artemis in the Battle of
the Gods and Giants,' stone relief, Archaeological Museum, Delphi.

The author wishes to thank Jean Davies, Jack David, Scott
Mitchell, and Robert Lecker for their guidance and support.
Thanks to Yehuda Miklaf for advice on Hebrew etymology.

Set in Caslon by ECW Type & Art, Oakville, Ontario.
Printed by The Porcupine's Quill, Erin, Ontario.

Distributed in Canada by General Distribution
Services, and in the United States by Login.

Published by ECW PRESS, 2120 Queen Street East,
Suite 200, Toronto, Ontario, Canada M4E 1E2.

For Mercy has a human heart,
Pity, a human face,
And Love, the human form divine,
And Peace, the human dress.

William Blake, *Songs of Innocence*

Prologue

I have spent most of my time in creation alone. I have been known to many, revered by great multitudes, but loved by scant few. This story is the true history of someone who loved me in their heart, and whom I loved in return. The facts of this tale are known to me because I attended their course as they unfolded. I am moved to offer these details, where she cannot, for their value to me, and for no other reason. I speak the tale with the certain knowledge of her voice, from her person, where and as it took place; and in doing so have diligently attempted to make it faithful to an age in which, and to which, I am a stranger. She was called Grace. I have once been called Leucippe, mistakenly as Aganippe, later, and often, Epona, and, to my friend Grace, Amor.

Tell me, some pitying angel, tell, quickly say,
Where does my soul's sweet darling stay,
In tigers', or more cruel Herod's way?
Ah! rather let his little footsteps press
Unregarded through the wilderness,
Where milder savages resort;
The desert's safer than a tyrant's court.
Why, fairest object of my love,
Why dost thou from my longing eyes remove?
Was it a waking dream, that did foretell
Thy wondrous birth? No vision from above?
Where's Gabriel now, that visited my cell?
I call: 'Gabriel! Gabriel! Gabriel! Gabriel!'
He comes not. Flatt'ring hopes, farewell.

from The Blessed Virgin's Expostulation
by Natham Tate, after Luke 2:42, for Henry Purcell
(Harmonia sacra, *book II, London, 1631)*

L ook at your hands!' I heard myself say. I didn't think before saying it, and there was no one to hear me anyway. The thought arose on its own, from something I had read many years before. A touchstone, left in storage for use at a specific future time and place, now recovered and spoken to darkness. Even as I said it I was trying to recall where I had collected the impulse. It was a technique, an embedded caprice, an automatic response to mobilize the mind at the instant you found yourself aware in a dream. The idea was that if you performed a directed action at that moment, you could or would leap to full sensibility. I suppose one's own hands were the only things considered reliably available for the exercise.

Without pausing to weigh the sense of it, I looked down and raised my open hands. There they were, outlined with a smooth silver lustre. But I did not detect any other transformation in myself or my thinking on the instant. I was just there, looking at my palms.

This couldn't be a dream, I decided, simply because I've never wondered at the time if a dream is a dream or not. Dreams I tend to muddle through, informed at some elementary level that they are a thing apart from my regular life. Not that I know what a dream might actually *be* in clear objective terms. It is more a set of friendly assumptions than a box of hard facts. But then the same is true of the huge whole universe. Our understanding is persistently limited to present best assumptions.

It passed through my mind that I might be dead, at which I hoped that I had said the name of God at the moment I had gone. Like Gandhi, clearly heard to intone 'RAM' a single second after he was shot. A Hindu's automatic response for deliverance to heaven.

But then I thought, if I'm thinking this and can see my hands, I'm not dead. 'Descartes to the rescue,' I said aloud.

Of course there's dead and there's DEAD. Sleeping and dreaming I might be 'dead to the world,' but that's hardly lifeless. How could I know anything about really *dying* yet? — 'Taking the long dirt nap' my granddad used to say! — I certainly didn't know what the afterworld might be like, or even if there *was* one. There, as I looked at my hands, it was just dark. Not warm or cold. I was not sitting or standing. I was just there, in the dark, confused.

I had other expectations of heaven.

As the moments passed I felt like I must be waking from a deep sleep — collecting the instruments of my being out of a stupor, if you like. I was puzzled, but not afraid. Some amount of fear would have been natural, I suppose, but I just didn't perceive any particular threat, apart from being disoriented. The disturbing confusion of failing to locate oneself.

I *struggled* to make better sense of things, ordering my thoughts with a fresh summary of the problem. I had suddenly appeared there, I said to myself. I may well have been sleeping, but I could not remember when or where I lay down to rest, and I did not awaken to find myself anywhere familiar.

It wasn't hell. I could hear music. I didn't think there would be music in hell. It was a song, a voice.

I could see better after a few minutes. My eyes were adjusting to the dark, and, I believed, the darkness was actually lifting.

Sunrise! I thought. I was so glad it was sunrise. The time of day I have always loved best. When I was younger I often went out in the morning before sunrise — something which a young woman might be advised against now, in the city anyway. I was always fascinated with the low light of early dawn, and was pleasantly energized by the bright morning sun when it appeared over the horizon.

Bright sunsets just gave me a headache. Still do.

But I could see this was the first dull light of a new day.

Not much emerged from the night. A long expanse ahead, with large dark patches off in the distance to either side — rolling hills, I thought, bordering a broad plain. Maybe a prehistoric glacial trough, now long eroded, and level across its expanse with the packing of thousands of years of sediment.

This contemplation of the landscape was just a few moments' refuge I took from my perplexity. A second later I shrank again, and shouted out loud in exasperation. 'What — is — going — on!' Even as I paced my words slowly, with great concluding emphasis, nobody answered.

It looked like there was frost in the air. I saw it *was* frost. It is cold, I thought. I did not *feel* cold. I looked down, and could see that there was fresh snow on the ground. I also saw that I was standing. I realized that I must have been motionless for — well, for as long as I'd been aware I was there.

I took a step, meeting the firm ground below, but without disturbing the snow, and leaving no hollow where my foot had been. And WHAT was this thing I was wearing? A long dress, all in black.

Just a dream, I thought. It must be a dream.

I remembered a *Twilight Zone* episode I'd seen several months back. It wasn't any longer than that, I said to myself — it was only three years ago, I think, in 1959, that the second channel started up in Edmonton. In the show this man suddenly finds himself in a distant place. A place from his own past, in the Sahara desert, where he had crashed a heavy bomber during the war. His psyche so badly needed to redeem the death of his colleagues that he actually went back to the time and place at which the tragedy had occurred — or so the program suggested.

But his feet left prints in the sand. And he sweated in the hot desert sun.

And he didn't hear bits of singing in the air. I hope I've not gone insane, I thought. Or had a massive stroke or something. It was just one voice, very pleasant, though I couldn't make out the lyrics. I thought it must be a tenor — a heldentenor! Wisps of heroic songs, but they were not Wagner.

Then, as I was busy wondering about my footprintless step and straining to hear the song better, my gaze was arrested by *movement* — just a few yards in front of me!

My heart was suddenly gripped with fear. That particular dread which grows with every breath, escalating as more and more of your being in turn focusses on the object of sudden alarm.

What I saw was a *man* suddenly rising out of the smooth snow cover! The same way the army of men rose out of the earth from the dragon's teeth Jason sowed in his trial. He was nearly naked — visibly strong, on the short side, with a rugged Mediterranean complexion colouring the chiselled features of middle age. He sat up, careless of the snow covering him; then stood, turned, and gazed all about him.

My panic eased when I was content that he was, indeed, human — and that he seemed to take no notice of me. He recovered an axe from beneath the snow, and started to split some wood.

I no sooner had another blurt of starts, when other men began appearing from the snow! Heads and hands and elbows and knees were popping up almost as far as I could see. Suddenly it was *just* like Jason! Except that these men were tattered, drowsy, and cold. Some were in undergarments, others in full attire. Wartime attire, tunics and armour and the like. Ancient armour.

I realized then — it just came to me, and with some relief — that these men had slept on the ground, and there had been a heavy snow during the night. The snow cover would have kept them warm, and would also have discouraged them from getting up, out to the open air where it was colder.

One of them called to the man that had gotten up first. In Greek — old Greek! Well, girl, I said to myself, you never thought that Classics would be of any use — it certainly wasn't much to swell your pride as a teacher at Crestwood elementary school — but that knowledge may now just save your life. I was tense with excitement that I could understand the better part of what he was saying!

And then in a trice I was overcome with despair. Could I be animating some kind of horrible hallucination? Had I suffered a seizure, and was my mind now seeking sanctuary in a familiar historical narrative? I was filled with anxiety at the possibility. Did my granddad return to the old Scottish croft after his attack, when we all thought he was just sitting in his chair day after day, senseless? No. No, I don't think so.

'Commander!' one of the men said in Greek. 'Sir! . . . Xenophon, sir! You inspire us with your resolve this cold morning.'

Xenophon! I thought. Getting up out of the snow half naked and chopping wood! Suddenly I knew exactly where I was. And when.

'But it can't be *real*,' I said.

I was spirited again as I watched the bivouac coming to order for the day. I'm really there! I thought. How could it be? All of this took place about 400 B.C. Maybe somebody is making a movie.

I strained to look closer, to see more clearly. No, whatever it is, I thought, it's not an entertainment. These guys don't just *look* like ancient-world Greek soldiers, they really *are* ancient-world Greek soldiers. If this is Xenophon in the snow, I think this camp must be in south-east Turkey. Near the source water of the Tigris.

I was relieved to have some bearings, so much so that I made a tacit agreement with myself, to accept them as given for the moment, even if rationally incomprehensible.

The soldiers began raising an awful odour, smearing themselves with lard — hog's lard, I heard someone say — and turpentine, mixed with other smelly stuff, like bitter almond. At home they would have 'washed' with olive oil. But they were a long way from home — as I was, I thought — and I guess this was the best they could do. Not that their mixture was any more improbable than lye and soda ash, or whatever it is we combine for soap.

I noticed that there was a scrub wood a short way behind where I was standing. Several sheep and oxen belonging to the army were tethered there, and a free-grazing horse. A good distance further beyond that I thought I could see some dwellings, or large tents.

As I gazed around, I suddenly caught the horse's glance, and was chilled and anxious as it stared back at me. The sun was not yet fully in view, and in the dim light everything was subdued — but I could see a distinct, unnatural red glint in its eye.

That chill deepened as I understood that the beast *was* looking at me.

M any fires were lit, and the camp was soon alert with activity. I was astonished at how one man appearing from under the snow could grow so quickly into this carnival of exertion. I had some trouble taking in the full commotion, probably because I was grasping for too many answers to too many questions at once. I had hardly budged from the spot where I first found myself.

It was not hard to determine the general drift of goings-on. After the men were warmed by their fires, and had smeared themselves with their noisome ointment, they attired and milled about, finding their way into their respective squadrons. Through this they were soft-tempered — the low rumble of thousands of muttering voices, an acre or more of hale bodies stretching and slapping and rubbing themselves in the cold air, with the light clank of armour, shields, spears, and swords.

There was little laughter — although I did not hear much complaining either. I thought these soldiers must be rugged, mentally and physically, in a way that men and women in my day have long lost and forgotten. Their faces were weathered from a lifetime out of doors — like the faces of plains Indians in photos taken before their territories were overrun with Europeans. Poignant and compelling landscapes in skin.

I multiplied in my mind the rough bulk of the one thousand students at my school, when they were gathered for assembly in the auditorium, and estimated a handful better than nine thousand soldiers present here. That may seem like a lot, but it was not a huge number for a legion in the ancient world.

The men were assembled in companies mainly on the basis of their armaments. The groups here were, I thought, a common assortment for the Greeks: mostly light-armoured peltasts, armed with a javelin and small shield, hoplites, the heavy-armoured infantry, and some archers and slingers. They were not generally in prime condition, as near as I could tell. A battered army making an unhappy, protracted escape from an unsuccessful mission.

I could hear the captains raising shouts, to organize their labour. Food was, apparently, the first order of business.

As the division chiefs hollered their instructions, I was struggling with a certain behest of my own — to remember how Xenophon's story went. Why couldn't this be Hannibal! *That* story I knew intimately! Or Aeneas — Virgil I had just about memorized. Oh God, how did this one go? I read Xenophon only once, in English — a translation of *Anabasis* in (smoothed) prose, which I had in a little Penguin book, *The Persian Expedition*. I had a vivid picture in my mind of the bold black title on the flat orange and white banded cover. 'Think, girl, THINK!' I said to myself.

Oh my. I know it was originally the story of Cyrus the younger, the great man, who raised an army for a campaign into Persia.

14

Against the urging of Socrates, and only loosely on the advice of the Priestess at Delphi, Xenophon signed on to go. He was already respected in Greece as an intellectual, knowledgeable in civil and military affairs. I think it was that all went well until Cyrus was killed at Cunaxa, at which point the offensive fell apart — with the Greek army isolated deep in Persia, near Babylon, between the Euphrates and Tigris rivers. By their wits, the Greeks managed to hold Artaxerxes II, the King of Persia, to a standoff, and negotiated a truce under which they would be escorted by a unit of the barbarian army north out of the king's territory.

Xenophon emerged to lead the host after a treacherous double-cross, where Clearchus (who had taken over from Cyrus) and all his generals were murdered by their escort in one of the great betrayals of the ancient histories. I could remember that Xenophon managed to get everybody into and through Kurdiſtan, weathering much struggle, and negotiating a string of deals for their passage, but I could not recall the details. I knew that they were heading for the Black Sea. Xenophon would become the first Greek to come around that way and return home through the Bosporus and Byzantium, with the last remnants of the forces of the wise and generous Cyrus.

I could vividly recall reading how the 'Ten Thousand' — though, again, I don't think there were fully ten thousand remaining — at last made it to 'the sea, the sea!'

It wouldn't be accurate to say the horse spoke to me. That is, I heard it speak, but not like Mister Ed on television, say, with a flapping of horse gums and broad showings of teeth. I could just 'hear' what it said.

It appeared around from my left — suddenly, it seemed, but I had been focussed on the activity ahead of me, and hadn't noticed it approaching. Up close, its red eyes were warm, and I was, on the instant, strangely comforted.

'Can you see me?' it said in Greek.

'Yes,' I said, only mildly surprised hearing the beast speak.

'I have not seen anyone here for several weeks,' it said.

'But there are thousands of people about,' I said sheepishly.

'On this side,' the horse replied.

'I'm sorry, but I don't understand,' I said, and I began to cry. Not from anxiety — I was overwhelmed with relief, just speaking to someone. Even Mister Ed.

'Calm yourself,' the horse said.

A few minutes passed between us in silence. I looked away, blankly watching the soldiers. I gathered from what they were saying that the villages nearby were well stocked with provisions. Cattle, grain, dried fruits and vegetables, and wine. There's the Breakfast of Champions for you! I thought. Rare beef and strong wine. I grinned, and looked back at the horse. I felt a smile from it in return. I was so very glad to have a companion there.

'I am also happy for company,' the horse said, clearly understanding the look on my face. 'The last I knew briefly as an ally departed me a long time ago. I have taken my name from him. He was a great warrior in his own country, in another time. His name was Amor de Cosmos. I am now called Amor.'

'My name is Grace. Grace MacDuff.'

'Greetings to you, Grace.'

A chorus of whoops and hollers came up from the soldiers. They were moving off to take their supplies at the villages, to the north. It must have been discouraging for farmers and villagers in the old world, I thought. The impression you get from the histories is that their hard work was routinely surrendered to whatever army happened to be passing — that is, plundering — through. I suppose, on the other hand, that the armies travelled slowly, and that the campaigns were not so very numerous.

'They will not travel today,' Amor said. 'Some who strayed ahead last night saw fires in the distance. They will wait until night, and dispatch a reliable spy to determine the truth. They are now leaving the charge of the governor Tiribazus, of a territory of western Armenia, with whom the Commander concluded a treaty for passage. That bond entailed neither engaging the other, and that the Greeks could take provisions, provided no houses were burned. In neglect of orders, however, houses were burned the day before yesterday, after provisions were taken. Those involved were reprimanded; and, although Tiribazus has not broken his escort's distance, one mile behind, to take revenge, the Commander knows his situation is delicate.

'The night following the breach Xenophon's officers remained under cover at the villages, while the men slept out on the plain. Yesterday the whole army was brought together, and camped here last night, away from the town.'

'Are we in danger?' I asked.

'This is not the danger you may face,' he said — not altogether reassuringly. 'Climb on my back, and we will stay with the main party of the Greeks.'

Amor was enormous, and it was an effort to pull myself up, without any stirrups or anything. He was magnificent to look at, beautifully formed, black, long-maned, sleek, and muscular.

'Why can I touch you, and the earth seems solid underfoot, but we don't make holes in the snow?' I said when we were underway.

'We are on the same side,' Amor said. 'I cannot tell you of any scientific reason, only that this is the observation I have made.'

'*What* side? What do you mean?'

'You are a wraith,' he said. 'The ghost of someone not yet dead.'

I held Amor's mane for balance as we approached the hamlets at a lazy canter. I was bursting with questions after what he had said, but didn't want to spoil anything between us by seeming over-anxious.

The truth was, after hearing what Amor had to tell me, I was *very* anxious.

I had not become fearful; instead my mind was filled with worry. Touching Amor's strong back, or bringing my attention to the songs, the music, I would feel at ease. But as I might dwell on my thoughts, I would worry again. Wraith? A wraith?! Will I ever go home again? Will I die here? Why did this happen to me?

As we came closer, I could see that the mass of soldiers was about as large as the settlement, which itself was larger than I expected. The locus was a stately, windowed stone building, the size of a large country farmhouse, which the soldiers were calling 'the palace,' and which I assumed was the home of the local landlord. Dotted around the palace were a dozen villages, each hardly a stone's throw from the other and consisting of about fifty or more stout dwellings made of close knotted small timbers and thatch, together with two or three modest stone structures in a central compound. These appeared to be for the storage of foodstuffs — some were obviously granaries. Except that everything had a covering of beautiful fresh white snow, it was probably the bleakest estate I had ever seen. The locals were easy to tell from the Greeks, being generally a trifle shorter, darker skinned, and with more varied and colourful dress. The next thing to dirty rags, mind you, though a different kind of ragged from the Greeks — from farming rather than fighting.

The same kind of dirty as the foreigners, though. From not being washed.

The Armenians wore long shirts of rough wool, died and woven in close patterns, and brightly coloured but for the soiling and fading, with matching banded caps. The Greek cloaks were of the same sturdy weight, but made of a finer fabric in a single muted hue, fashioned to complement their various armours.

The Greek headgear was fascinating — often grimly beautiful; made of skilfully pounded bronze, in a variety of shapes and styles. Most had two large metal sideburns down around each cheek, a narrow opening in front for the eyes and nose, and a crest or plume. Others added a more prominent nosepiece, still others covered only the head, like a great drooped tam in metal, a few with hinged side flaps. They would need callused scalps under a good thick head of hair to wear any of them with any comfort, I thought.

The shouting raised when the Greeks went marching on their way had subsided. It was, I think, a device they used to rally their spirits, as well as to project a ferocious humour in battle. Here, however, they were being given food under their agreement with Tiribazus, so the tenor of things was more like an army field kitchen — a 'slum gun' my granddad used to say — than what I imagined would be the usual free-for-all. The Armenians were supplying dried fruits and legumes with some unleavened bread to each soldier. Most sat down to eat on the edge of town. Wine was being passed hand to hand in large vessels, from which each drank.

'Others will pack fresh meat, grain, and wine back to the fires at the main camp,' Amor said. 'The barley they will roast and crack, not bake, and the meat they will stake and broil. This will be their meal before dusk.'

Amor and I did not go into the crowded villages. Amor explained that, 'While we live in a world a step away from the world of men, we move among them and would, at times, be seen as shadows, or felt to collide with them.' He again said that he could not tell me any reason why. That was, he said, what he had observed.

His having come out with that, I felt at liberty to ask more. I thought I was handling my suspense and apprehension pretty well, but I wasn't going to miss any opportunity. Besides, I thought that talking with Amor would be comforting, no matter what was said. It was, although I found his formal way of speaking a little bit hard to understand.

'Are you also a wraith? How could you be here so long like that?' I said.

'I do not know what comedy governs my stay,' he replied, 'or what whim of The Creator may have committed me to this fate. Eight centuries ago I fell mortally wounded in a conflict of the Mycenae. I departed that spot in the condition you find me now, transparent to my former existence. Also, my reflexions and concerns of myself were changed. I began making observations, and knowing the nature and history of things; thoughts I did not know before. I have seen, however, that while there are a small number that will remain, as I have, most do not. They disappear, to rejoin their life, or to depart from it.'

'To depart from it?' I said. Although I knew full well what he meant, I put the question in the hope of more details. 'What do you mean?'

'I mean just that,' Amor replied, 'as the Goddess Night nurses the babe Sleep to one breast, and the babe Death to the other.'

'So I just hang around here, until I know if I'm alive or dead?'

'That is the truth, if you take no action. But it may be more prudent, if you wish to prolong your life in the corporeal, to act on your own behalf. From what country do you come?'

'From Canada,' I said. 'Well, I was born in England, in 1938, but then when the war started my mother brought me to Canada, to Edmonton, to escape. After the war —'

I stopped, as I had another thought break in.

'I'm sorry, Amor. You will not understand any of that, because what I am describing is not only another place, but another time in history. My life has been, or is, taking place hundreds of years from now! That must sound crazy.'

'Not at all. That is what I have observed to usually be the truth. As much as souls fall into this world, the twilight of creation, they fall from other lands and other situations, across the breadth of all dimensions. Once here, they are ruled by this time and place. I have heard about the two great wars of the world in the second millennia yet to come, and I have heard of the country Canada. The man from whom I took my name was a crusader in that country, when that country was in its infancy.'

'Can you hear the singing?' I asked quietly.

'What song is it you hear?' Amor said.

With that I had to stop and think. It wasn't simple, like telling someone you'd just heard 'I Got Rhythm' or 'Rock around the Clock' on the radio. Amor could see I wasn't sure what to say.

'The music is the current of this world, as all life vibrates in tone, and in turn is enveloped in tone. Pure tone, as simple as love, life, and death, and as complex as the vast weave of the universe.'

That sounded grand, but I knew he was just trying to explain.

'I hear a man singing. I'm sure now it's a heldentenor, but the song is not classical — what would be called classical in my time, that is.'

'I understand,' Amor said. He paused briefly, then continued. 'The music and the lives of men are in a close reciprocal relationship. For example, the great composers that have heard their harmonies in the air have been gifted to know the immaculate complex of this sphere in their hearts. And pure tone original of the hearts of great persons is also assimilated back into this vast ether, and known here. I cannot tell you why —'

'It is what you have observed,' I said, with the warmth of understanding in my voice.

Amor again paused for a second.

'The best I can tell you is this. What you hear is what your heart invites of its own nature. What form of voice or word it may assume is what your heart can understand. Whatever it may become, the music sustains you here, for you take no other nourishment.'

'I hear the same voice in different songs at different times — a pleasant, seamless changing. Does it mean something that they are heroic songs?'

20

Amor turned his head back sharply, so as to look at me squarely with one soft ruby eye. He said nothing, but I think I took his meaning clearly. *Take this simply, as it is.* It is just *me*, somehow, the sum of my life to now.

It happened that right then, for the first time, I could discern the lyric of the song for a second.

Like a bat out of hell I'll be gone when the morning comes.

I was going to tell Amor this, but he spoke up first and said, 'Let us not focus on the euphony for now. Our attention is due the commander Xenophon, as my devoted charge is to assist his safety. And, having arrived here, your fate is entwined with his, although in what full regard is not yet clear.'

What I observed next was the truth of an old maxim — what armies do mostly is wait. Travel, and wait. For Xenophon's men, tomorrow was for travel, today was to wait.

Ordinarily they probably would have passed a waiting day in drill, exercise, or cleaning and repairing their costumes and weaponry. These men, however, were now rather more depleted than that would demand. They weren't idle, but they weren't brisk about anything either.

After finishing their meal at the village, they marched back to the campsite where I had first seen them that morning. Five large orderly fire pits were constructed, arranged like the five-dotted side of a gambling die, about two hundred yards from corner-to-corner. The command post was established at the central fire; the outlying four served as gathering points and cooking fires. The lieutenants shouted orders as to which units were to assemble at which locations, and piles of supplies and foodstuffs were left adjacent to each. The fires burned brightly, and melted the snow to dry ground for several yards around.

And there they passed their day's leisure. Groups of men went from time to time to collect armsful of firewood at the scrub. Others dressed and spit the sides of oxen, which, I thought, would be at least a few hours cooking for that volume of meat. Others occupied themselves with vigorous walking, a few wrestling or sparring with their colleagues, some attending to the pack animals, which had been suffering terribly with the cold and snow. Still others stood and talked in low voices. The mood was staid, but not despairing.

Amor and I passed the afternoon walking quietly together. Most of the time I was happy just seeing it all, just being there. It was the same when I visited New York City two years ago — or rather, I should say twenty-three hundred years from now! — when I just walked around, wide-eyed, for a week.

Every so often I would erupt into horrible uneasiness, even being so engaged. Worrying about what was going to happen to me. How I was going to get home. Hoping dearly that I might wake up in my room, to find my roommate had brought a nice hot cocoa to my side table. She would tell me how hard I had been to wake up! And how she would have let me sleep in, except it was Saturday morning, and I had better get myself going. In the winter on Saturday mornings I give a dance class at the community centre. The kids are so sweet! All three- and four-year-olds, dressed in their little skirts and pink tights. Darling.

Those daydreams did not become real, however. Amor would notice my distant look from time to time, and nudge me gently with his nose, a sympathetic look in his eye, and I would reabsorb myself in the goings-on.

Amor was also passing the time quietly watching, but in no way wide-eyed. I guess he had been walking around taking in scenes like this for some time, and, whatever responsibility he had or felt, I'm sure there was little thrill left in it.

I wanted to ask him more about my situation, about what specific danger I might be in, and what I could do about it. There was restraint in my keeping quiet, but it was not an *effort* of restraint. I felt a peculiar assurance that he *would* speak up in his own time. That wasn't just because he was my only friend here — not only my only friend, but the only other living thing I had seen on this 'side'! — rather, I felt assured by every word he spoke, by every look he gave me.

I was not very good at estimating the time of day by the position of the sun, but Amor was experienced with these things. When the men lay out the barley to roast, he spoke up and said it was two hours before dusk. The barley would take about half an hour to brown and crack, and then they would eat, he said.

Their eating had a certain primæval quality about it, each taking their dripping hot share of meat on a stick, and tearing away at it with their teeth. They weren't vulgar about it, mind you; not, for example, how you might imagine the gluttons in decadent Rome to have been, a few centuries from now. I thought of Caligula for a second — though my intuition about him differed from the textbook account the professors repeated in class. I could not believe he was crazy or depraved. I think he was highly intelligent, sane, and, especially, must have had a highly developed sense of humour. His excesses (like the horse in the Senate) were his private satire of the corruption and decline he saw around him. Regardless, there was no Classics lecture, no textbook or theory, I thought, to equal my day today.

As their supper wound down, Amor pointed out to me that the Commander was calling his officials and advisors to conference, and we went over to join them. There were sixteen men present. Some were so *young*! Hardly twenty years old, I'm sure. Most were probably in their thirties, including Xenophon, a few others somewhat older. I remembered how all of the original generals had been murdered with Clearchus, so Xenophon had to recruit this mix from what people he had left.

I was disappointed that the talk progressed without any move to consult the viscera for guidance! My main recollection of Xenophon's narrative was the frequency with which he would call the seers and sages for advice. An ox would be slain, in order that its entrails could be examined as an oracle.

'No ox?' I whispered to Amor. Nobody would have heard if I spoke up, mind, but I whispered trying to show respect for Amor's concentration on the proceedings.

'They will not summon divine guidance at this council. You will see the ritual soon enough, I expect, and at that time ascertain its true relation to you and me.'

I didn't ask him to expand on that; though, as was becoming my habit, I wanted to.

Xenophon began his speech with a summary of their situation — how they were nearing their goal, and that they were newly past the grip of the King of Persia, although these lands were still subservient to his influence. He said that some individuals among them had blundered in reckless defiance of orders with the house burnings, bringing the whole party into fresh danger. Next he reminded them how some men had wandered ahead last evening, and seen fires in the distance. He then proposed that a single agent be sent now to investigate, and asked their assent.

All present thought this would be a good idea, and agreed they needed a determined officer of proven judgement and courage. Someone said that Democrates of Temenos would be just the man, having been utterly dependable on similar missions in the past; and all agreed. A servant was sent to find him.

Amor commented that the Greeks chose their leaders, not so much for their greatness in battle, but for their elocution, and powers of deduction and rational thought.

'This is the distinction they make between themselves and the barbarians,' he said. 'For the Greeks, the army is an ambulatory political forum as much as an instrument of war, and their leaders are elected for their skill at debate.'

The servant returned in about ten minutes' time, together with his charge. Democrates was a striking figure, about twenty years old, looking immensely strong, with a refined air about him. The two of them came up to join the council nearby where Amor and I were standing. As they passed by us, Democrates glanced in my direction. I could have sworn I saw a distinct double-take in his gesture. With the second glance he darted back I was certain he had looked me straight in the face. His eyes widened ever so slightly, and then the two of them carried on by. All in an instant.

'Amor, I think he could see me!' I said with undisguised surprise and distress.

'Yes,' Amor replied. 'I have had no previous contact with him, but I now believe this Democrates is a traveller.'

I noticed another pattern emerging in my new friendship with Amor. The horse says something. The girl finds the remark loaded with a thousand new questions. (He was the horse. I was the girl.) The number of questions swelled and swelled — though I *had* had just about all the answers I could digest, too.

This time Amor took up the slack a little right away, as the council was still in recess.

'It would be best if I do not tell you anything about the fate of humankind after your era, although I have some knowledge of those affairs. I believe you can grasp my intent in this regard. I will say only that your natural lifetime is perceived as a period of hysteria, waste, and ruin — growth without conscience, and sustained senseless destruction on the part of humankind. This was the fresh emergence of a progressive barbarism, veiled with sophisticated politics, refined speech, and technical skills.'

While Amor was speaking, we watched as Xenophon and his generals greeted Democrates, sat him down, and poured him wine. The music filled the crisp night air with singular brilliance. The song was simple, but of great beauty, I thought.

And a band of angels wrapped up in my heart.

'Then came a great wind-down,' Amor continued. 'Those who carried on, amidst other losses, inherited a wealth of technical achievement, one notably in the mechanics of the ether.'

'You mean moving in time?!' I blurted out, anticipating him, and laughed. 'Amor, that's daft! Impossible!'

'There is such a technique, and I have been told it is at once more complex than you can imagine, and, in its use, simpler than you might suppose. This you might understand more fully by example. In your time you have at your disposal any number of implements and machines which these soldiers would utterly fail to comprehend, while their application to you is uncomplicated.'

'That is true,' I said. 'And there are many things that I know how to use, but I haven't taken the time to learn how they actually work. Like the television, or the engine in my car.'

Our time for chat was running short, as it was clear the meeting was going to resume shortly.

'Suffice it to say that, whatever their exact means, the travellers are in the world of men, and bodily traverse the gossamer with their invention. There are only a few that gained this inheritance, and they have not been active long, in terms of spent time. They are, however, well known by story and reputation to those equal few, such as me, marooned in this world. A consequence of their mobility in time is the ability to see and hear over the boundary.'

So Democrates must have been startled to see an unexpected face in the crowd. Or it may have been the clothes! At this, I looked to my knees, and gazed at the billowing black dress I arrived here wearing. With the shoulder cloak, I thought I looked like a witch. I looked up at Amor.

'Don't they change the future, then?' I asked.

'There is only one prospect for the world. What the travellers do at this place and time has, in your blithe life ahead, already taken place, and in only one way. Wherever they range, their endeavours contribute the same part as any mortal soul to the great constellation of events. You, in your history, already know the deed and consequence of every breath drawn by every traveller gone before you. There is only one outcome.'

I had to think about that for a second. They haven't been changing anything. They are instead a part of what happened when it happened, the one time it happened.

Xenophon was beginning to speak. He welcomed Democrates, praising his courage and reputation for reliability. He said that he had sent for him to accomplish a mission of importance.

'Can one of them go and see if I am okay, or what has become of me, in the future?' I whispered.

'Why, yes, perhaps they can,' Amor answered. He said it considering his words as they were spoken.

After Democrates had been instructed by Xenophon, the meeting was adjourned. He was to leave that night with a small detachment, and, under cover of darkness, investigate the reports of fires. Fires meant men — albeit men investing little effort to disguise their presence — and men meant the possibility of an ambush.

As Democrates came back past us, he gestured to Amor with a little tilt of the head — meaning that we should follow him.

'He *can* certainly see us,' I said quietly.

'Yes,' Amor replied, 'and you may rest assured that his purposes are honourable and benevolent.'

I pulled myself up onto Amor's back and we rode off slowly, keeping Democrates and his entourage in sight. They made their way to one of the outlying campfires, and Democrates proceeded to select about thirty men to come with him. Most were hoplites, chosen for their bodily strength and vigour. He told them to reduce their heavy armour in the interest of stealth, and their hypaspists — the slaves that accompanied them in the field, assisting with their gear — were to remain behind. No engagement was expected, but Democrates wanted men capable of rolling large stones should the need arise.

While the commandos he selected were busy with their preparations, Democrates came over to where we were standing, horse and rider, to discreetly say a few words. He held his face down, wiping his mouth with a rag to disguise his speaking. Otherwise, to anyone happening to notice, he would have been talking to empty air.

'We will not have any good chance to speak tonight. Tomorrow, before midday, when I go to rest.' And, having hardly broken his gait, he continued on his way.

Within the half hour they were on their way north.

We followed his party for a time on their mission. It was a strange feeling, knowing that we were safe from the danger that threatened these men, that we could wander and observe anything we wished, and didn't get cold or hungry.

Once past the villages where the army had collected their provisions earlier that day, the plain converged sharply into the hills. The moon was only the first night past new — contributing to the depth of darkness I had arrived in, I thought — and we couldn't see for any great distance. The faraway shadows, however, suggested that these hills turned into a barrier of mountains only a few miles further up the road.

There was little going on as we walked, two miles north of the villages and a hundred yards behind Democrates, so I spoke up.

'Amor, what danger am I in?'

'You may not be in danger,' he answered, 'if it is your fate to wander here as a ghost for time obscure. It is more usual, however, that your connexion with the world of men remains vital, and the energy available to you is limited. If the situation is typical, your spirit has been shed over the boundary on account of trauma or injury to your corporeal part. If that part is restored to health or comfort, then it will beckon you back. This is a thing of nature. Should it expire, your time here will finish, and you will pass on. This also is a thing of nature.'

'To where, Amor? Is there heaven?'

'I do not know. There is no more to observe of heaven, or any other certainty past the grave, here on this side, than there is anywhere in the world.'

'Can I not rejoin my body, to help it recover in some way?'

'I have not observed this to take place as a matter of will, though such a thing may have assisted many who in time have perished here. For others it would not have been any help, on account of the unfortunate state of their remains.'

E arly the next morning, before the army had risen, Democrates returned with his men. They had taken a prisoner.

The army had again slept out in the open. They were spared another covering of snow, though there were still several inches underfoot. Democrates marched straight over to where Xenophon was lying. He knelt down beside him, and shook his arm.

'The commander Xenophon has made it known to his men that any one among them may approach him at any time, day or night, if he has a message of importance,' Amor said.

Xenophon was as good as his word. I was astonished at how quickly he could bring himself to full composure and alertness, and in apparent good spirits. He sat up immediately, and welcomed Democrates warmly, asking how the task had gone. As though he had already read the paper over a couple of cups of coffee, followed by a good brisk morning walk.

'It went well, sir,' Democrates said. 'Attire yourself, and attend me to my men for an interview.'

Democrates' Greek, like my own, was a little stilted. I knew he was a traveller, of course, and not native to this place, though I did not really understand where he travelled to or from. By now, however, I was reconciled to getting along with a steady heap of questions. At least I hadn't been worrying so much since Amor told me what he had about Democrates. Or maybe I just wasn't worrying about the same things! I had begun to worry about my body, mostly. Was I dying? Had I had a been hit by a bus? Could I be lying in the snow somewhere at home, bleeding to death?

Oh my, oh my, oh my, I would say to myself. These thoughts could really get me worked up. Regardless, having a second contact, one in the 'real' world, was a great comfort. Whenever I found I was becoming distraught I would try to concentrate on the music. *Objects in the rear view mirror may appear closer than they are.* The voice was pure, and utterly beautiful. I had never heard any of the songs before, so I did not know the tunes or the lyrics. That lent a sense of discovery to what I heard, and encouraged me to listen carefully. Like most heroic songs, they were mostly stories about love — lost loves, sacrifices for love, courage in the face of disappointed love, hope for renewed love, and that sort of thing. I guess it meant that I was a great romantic, if this was the music I attracted! Well, I knew I was a romantic; but, while my memory of my life in the world was not complete, I knew in my heart that I was a *failed* romantic. It wasn't that I was bad looking or anything, I don't think. No, I was pretty enough, and I was careful about putting myself together nicely. I didn't use much makeup, just a little powder and lipstick.

It was instead that I never learned how to speak to men. My girlfriend, my roommate, Faith, always says that I show too much enthusiasm if I like a man, and that scares them off. I sure would like to see Faith now, I thought. My mother always joked about our names. 'Now if we had Hope and Charity staying in this house, we would have most of the Christian virtues under one roof!'

A sad smile came to my lips, and I wished I could see my mother now too. If I am in trouble at home, she will be very worried.

Amor shook his head from side to side and shuffled his feet, as horses do, somehow aware of my thoughts. I patted his broad neck, and returned my attention to the Greeks.

As Democrates returned with Xenophon to meet the reconnaissance party, the prisoner lay himself out flat on the ground.

'This indicates he is Persian,' Amor said. 'They prostrate their persons when they come into the presence of men of authority, as a sign of subservience.'

'Stand up and face me,' Xenophon sternly instructed him.

'The Greeks regard this custom with disdain,' Amor added, 'they themselves make this devotion exclusively to the Gods, and never to men.'

'This villain was captured in the hills, by Cleon and Deodotus, with this bow, quiver, and axe,' Democrates said. 'While the axe is one carried by the Amazons, the bow is assuredly Persian.'

'What is your country?' Xenophon asked, 'and under whose command and on what mission do you skulk in the darkness?'

The man said, 'I am Persian, of an army of the Armenian territory. I have been sent by Tiribazus to find provisions.'

'Tiribazus established his camp one mile south of here three days ago. What army is it now ensconced in the land to the north, in the mountains, and for what nefarious purpose has it been assembled?' Democrates demanded.

The prisoner said that Tiribazus had sent some of his own men around the Greeks to new positions ahead of this campsite, to the north, along the path of their march to the sea. As well, he had hired mercenaries from the Chalybes and Taochi. They all lay in wait in the mountains, prepared to attack the Greeks as they passed. There was, apparently, one stretch where the only way through was a narrow pass. They would be an easy target — 'sitting ducks,' my granddad would say.

Xenophon had that look in his eye, of someone who wasn't going to stand for this. Of someone who could never accept treachery as a way of life. Then his face softened a little. I sensed he must be considering how Tiribazus would have found the house burnings at the townsite to be treacherous.

Then he furrowed his brow, and drew his lips taut. I imagined then he was thinking that, while each party may feel betrayed, it remained that he had to get himself and the Ten Thousand out of here, whatever the details or complexities.

And then he acted. Most of the men were still sleeping on the packed snow, but not for long. Xenophon walked smartly back to the central firesite and shook his generals, calling them by name.

'Collect your men!' he was saying. 'We bring the army to battle today! Collect your men!'

For me, a gentle schoolteacher, this would not have been very good news, especially first thing in the morning. I could see, however, that battle is what gave these men purpose — past the debate, past their causes, past their needs, it seemed to me then that battle was the material expression of their polity. This is how I read their faces: at once galvanized with purpose. Connecting the real and the hypothetical.

Preparations still went in turn. The campfires were re-lit, and the soldiers again warmed themselves, smeared their persons with lard and turpentine, and ate cold ox meat with some wine before donning their battle gear.

I did not perceive the quick order they made into ranks as conformity or servitude. It struck me as a combination of individual pride and belonging, together with the knowledge that their redemption was only going to be as a disciplined whole.

Amor and I watched them in silence. I was riding on his back so we could move and act together without hesitation — something done without any discussion, in such a way as I felt we were already beginning to grow close to one another.

He was a lovable mix, I thought, of warm, encouraging, and supportive gestures, together with his very reserved way of speaking. I often had to remind myself that he *was* a horse, and not a person; and had, as he described it to me, only leapt to his present awareness on crossing the boundary.

'Have you seen any other beast on this side, Amor?' I asked.

'Yes, I have observed a number of others, but I am the only one I have seen possessed of rational sense.'

'You must have been the soul of a man,' I said, a little surprised at my own boldness.

Amor said nothing, but swung his head around with a grin in one red eye.

'What do you love, Amor?'

'You would find my passions to be bland, Grace,' he responded. 'My time here is bland, of limited moment to either world. There is little I can do but observe, and acquire knowledge that comes to little result.'

'You are enriching my life, Amor. That may be a modest result, but it is as large as all the love one can give.' After saying this, I blushed, and was afraid Amor would find it maudlin.

'That is the first sincere gratitude ever paid to me, Grace.'

As midday approached, and the men were nearly ready to march to battle, Amor and I went looking for Democrates. He had laid down to rest in the soft snow of scrub wood, alongside another soldier.

The sun was bright, though it must have been cool, judging by the red cheeks and knees that we passed on our way to the wood. Democrates sat up, resting on his hands, when we approached.

'You may speak freely in the presence and company of my good friend here. You must be Amor, the famous steed of the twilight. And you?' he said, with a gesture in my direction.

'Grace MacDuff,' I said, 'from Canada, in the middle of the twentieth century.'

'Oh, Canada?' Democrates said pleasantly. 'A long way and span from home I see.'

'I have only been here a short time.'

'Yes, I can tell from the vigour in your eyes,' he replied. 'My name is Arthur, and this is Margaret, whom the Greeks call Chalus.'

'Margaret!' I said. 'You are a woman!' What I was seeing, so to speak, was a menacing light-armoured slinger.

'I am disguised as a man for this journey,' she said, and removed her helmet. I gasped with a peculiar vague recognition.

'Do I know you?' I said. 'You look so familiar!'

'No, I don't think so,' she said, and smiled.

Democrates, or rather, Arthur — I decided I should call him by his real name — then said, 'Our time now is short, as the march will begin soon. Let me tell you our story, and then I hope Grace will tell us her own. Amor the horse I know by reputation, and I am very glad to see you now.'

He paused, collecting his thoughts.

'As you may know, Amor and Grace, we are two of the original twelve who had a slip device implanted in their bodies two years in travelled time ago. We are both twenty-two years of age. There were four of us together when we first came to this time, but one was killed in battle when Cyrus was still in command. His name was Gerald, and we mourn his loss. The fourth, another woman, is too slight and dark skinned to have masqueraded as a Greek, so she slipped ahead, and we expect to rejoin her at Trapezus, the Greek town on the Black Sea, which is the objective of this march.'

'How could Gerald be killed if you are travellers?' I asked naïvely.

'We are human beings,' Arthur said, 'no different in any way from you in your normal life. This travelling is not a science fiction story of riddles and paradoxes and supranormal activity. We are living our lives the same as you, getting older day by day, and subject to every illness, risk, and death. The *only* difference is that we can begin our next day in a different place, and a different place in time, having the slip device. Otherwise, our lives move ahead in a straight line, and our bodies age as time goes by. Natural laws are observed, of course, laws in addition to those you are familiar with. These prevent our being in two places at once, for example, just as we cannot pass clean through a stone wall, or jump to the moon.'

'I understand,' I said, 'and Amor has already explained to me how you are not changing anything, that you are a part of history as it takes place. Even if you step suddenly into various times and situations.'

'That is correct. Besides, there were only twelve of us, hardly a multitude in the huge mass of mankind. Our lives are short, and our interests have been directed more toward uncovering ancient knowledge than emending modern history.'

'What kinds of things have you done?' I asked, aware that I was using up valuable time with a question that could wait.

'We have seen the giant reptiles and dinosaurs, before man — one of us slipped to the Cambrian, against the advice of the rest, and we fear he is lost. We have seen early man, Neanderthal, and Cro-Magnon. And the giants, mentioned in Genesis, whose bones were discovered by the Spartan Benefactor Lichas. Many times and places. In our hearts, we have been looking for the spirit of God.'

'Have you found him?' Really I was wondering if *I* was going to find him if I didn't get back home.

'Before coming here to Asia Minor, we went to find Job, not knowing what part was legend and what part was truth. That was the last time *Yahweh*, whom others call *'Elohim*, was said to speak. Allow me to tell you more details another time. That, then, has been the substance of our careers. How have you come here, Grace MacDuff?'

'I just arrived, suddenly, the day before yesterday. I'm afraid my old self is in some terrible trouble, and I don't know what to do about it!' Without wanting to, I drew my breath in a sob.

'I see that you are in distress, Grace, and I pledge that Margaret and I will assist you if we can, and I hope and believe that we can rely on you to assist us in our difficulty.'

33

'And what *is* that peril?' Amor asked.

'Our travel here was originally planned as an adventure, to participate in this important event of the ancient world. We misjudged the terrible danger and hardship that it entailed, however, including, as I mentioned, the death of our brother. We have to conclude this march, or lose touch with Elizabeth, now waiting for us at the sea. Being so few, and being so very distant from our home, there is a close bond between us. But there is more to our trouble than that. Gerald had on his person a gift, given him by Job when we left. It is a ring, which was taken from his hand by another soldier when he was slain. We have been looking for the soldier with our ring on his hand, but without success; and, even when we find him, we need a plan to recover it. Without murder.'

'This ring may turn out to be of some assistance to *you*, Grace,' Margaret said. 'Job was much concerned with the world you inhabit now, over the boundary, as God had spoken to him over that same verge. When he gave us the ring he said, *This is the bridge.* He offered no further explanation, and we have been unable to understand what manner of talisman or instrument it is. Perhaps you might know.'

'Me?' I said quietly.

'Something may occur to you, from your history and education, that we failed to see.'

'We must join our ranks now,' Arthur said. As he rose to leave, I caught my reflexion in his shield — their possessions also bridged our worlds, somehow — and let out a gasp, from shock! My face was older, and wrinkled, and my eyes were red, like Amor's!

'It is always Hallowe'en over the boundary!' Arthur said, laughing warmly. 'Little children often can see over, and tell of ghosts and goblins.'

A guard was left at the camp, three hundred men under the command of Sophænetus the Stymphalian. The rest marched ahead to battle, toward the mountains — the peltasts in front, and the hoplites, including Xenophon, who was heavily armed, behind. Arthur and Margaret were in the forward party.

As the march proceeded, the peltasts moved farther and farther ahead, having much lighter loads. Amor and I stayed back with the hoplites. Early in the afternoon we arrived at the edge of the mountains, knowing that the others were now well ahead of us.

Suddenly we heard a ferocious noise on the wind, the roar of thousands of peltasts raising shouts of battle. We were riding beside Xenophon. I could see he was distressed at the shouts, wondering if his generals had wisely decided to attack, or if they had been ambushed.

Xenophon stepped up the march, as much as he could. Even these great hulks could not go very fast packing the weight they were. They were like walking Woodward's appliance floors. Within the hour, however, messengers came back from the front.

They found Xenophon at the head of the column of hoplites. He told them to rest their breath for a moment, and report.

'Glad news of victory,' one said. 'The peltasts came within sight of the enemy camp. The general Nicoſtraton said they had the advantage in this landscape, and would not wait for the hoplites. He gave the order to attack, and we swooped down on the barbarians with loud shouts. The natives were immediately unnerved, and fled. Some we killed in flight. As well, we took the command tent used by Tiribazus, together with three horses.'

'Some of your buddies,' I said to Amor.

'Yes, but they are as I was before — with emotion in their heart, but without deductive observation or recollection.'

Another of the men produced a small silver vessel, saying, 'We bring you Tiribazus' goblet, and there are other artifacts, including silver-legged couches. As well, there are prisoners from among his servants, including his bakers and cup-bearers.'

Xenophon waved for the trumpets to be sounded, to order the men back to camp. Although their slender horns could only produce three notes, they had a varied repertoire of signalling rhythms.

Before nightfall the entire group was back. The guard had heard the trumpets signalling the army's return, and had re-lit the fires. Some sheep had been slaughtered, and were roasting on spits.

I remarked to Amor that it had been a full day.

'They will have to march vigorously tomorrow, to get clear of the pass before Tiribazus can regroup.'

Arthur and Margaret passed by us in the crowd, and I smiled to show I was happy they were okay. Arthur returned a wink.

35

He came over closer, pulled a rag to his nose, as before, and said, 'Staying here, even one day more, is begging trouble. This army has to hop to and clear out. Can you do anything, Amor? You know these Greeks are so superstitious that a sneeze will bring them to their knees, thanking the Gods for giving them a sign.'

I was amazed with what Amor did next!

He asked me to climb off his back, and trotted over to the sheep spit at Xenophon's fire, fifteen or twenty yards away, where a whole animal was turning. He turned, facing away from the sheep, rocked forward — and then with a *fantastic* blow, drove his rear hooves into the carcass. More from celestial shock than contact, its entrails spilled out onto the ground.

The Greeks were *stunned*. Frozen. Silent. Statues of men with wide eyes and dropped jaws. And then they all, to a man, dropped face down on the ground.

Then Xenophon stood up. In a firm voice he told the armoured carpet of men at his feet that they had witnessed divine guidance. They would march tomorrow at the first light.

'I have been the oracle for this tragic expedition since it began,' Amor said.

Through the night, Amor and I stayed with Margaret and Arthur. Shortly before dawn, Arthur looked over toward us. With a genial, furtive wave he suggested we come closer.

'I feel less lonely having made two new friends,' Arthur said quietly, 'though our acquaintance may be short. Most any amity is fleeting for us, while we travel. But, even with that, and our other hardships, I believe this adventure has been worthwhile. Except for the death of our colleague. He may otherwise have passed away in some inconsequential accident at home, of course. I'm sure he would not have expressed regret for making the journey.'

'No, I don't think he would have,' I said.

'I am happy at least that he is not having to sleep on this cold, wet ground,' Arthur added, lightening the mood.

'Can you hear the music, Grace?' Margaret asked.

'Why, yes I can! Do you?'

'Sometimes we can hear, but only occasionally, and only if all around is very still. What harmony do you hear?'

'I do not recognize it.'

'They are the songs of a heldentenor in Grace's ear,' Amor said.

'What song do you hear now, Grace.'

'Um,' I said, 'I cannot sing it! *I want you, I need you, but there ain't no way I'm ever gonna love you,*' I recited, feeling slightly foolish. It was so *flat* said like that.

'But two out of three ain't bad!' Arthur said, smiling broadly.

'That's right!' I said, unsure if he had simply guessed at it.

'That is a popular song from your era, Grace, — or rather, twenty-five or thirty years after this recess from your natural life at mid-century. You may also have heard that *Heaven can wait*, or perhaps of *Where angels sing?*'

'Yes, I have!' I said, now amazed at his knowledge.

'Some might find it unlikely or odd,' Arthur said, 'but it truly happened that one of the great tenors of that century chose to perform popular songs. He was under-appreciated by his contemporaries as a result, but come our day, in the next, was celebrated for his exceptional skill. If his voice sounds in the ether, I should perhaps say his transcendent skill.'

'What is his name?' I said.

'Meat Loaf,' Margaret replied.

At that, Amor made a rapid wheezing sound through his nostrils, and shook his head.

I think this must have been a laugh! He hadn't shown any particular sense of humour up to then, but I guess that drew him out. I laughed then too, and so did Arthur and Margaret, though they held their nostrils, so as to make as little noise as possible.

'I think Mr. Loaf must have intended his choice to have a comic aspect,' Amor remarked. 'Such a thing is strengthening.'

'A well-respected artist,' Arthur added, 'and a *singular* voice.'

'Yes,' I said.

D awn was showing itself, and the morning preparations were getting under way. Margaret and Arthur groomed themselves with lard, then went to collect firewood. The extra winter garments they needed made disguising Margaret much easier, I thought.

The soldiers were moving along faster than they had the past two mornings, and were ready to move out in no time.

It had snowed again in the mountains, adding several inches to the already substantial accumulation on the ground north of the villages. Three people were taken from the town against their will, to serve as guides, on the promise they would be released when they had delivered the army through the pass. If they led them astray, they would be promptly slaughtered.

We went the same way as the day before, going to battle, but this time the whole troupe was moving — soldiers, slaves, servants, pack animals, and livestock. Whereas yesterday the hoplites had lagged behind, today it was the baggage cattle. They could handle a tremendous weight, I could see, but they weren't easy to keep moving, or to direct. Sometimes they would panic and bolt, or fall with frozen hoofs and spill their loads.

One-third or more of the force was armed and ready to defend the rest against ambush. Those not mobilized at any given time were packing loads of gear and supplies, or assisting with the animals. As they came off the last of the plain, into the mountains, the going was increasingly more difficult.

I could hear some of the peltasts calling to point out the place where they had come down on the natives, and driven them away. There were a number of corpses lying about, apparently, to verify their story, but I was not interested to see.

Darkness was falling as we came through the pass, just a short way along from the heights where Tiribazus had planned to make his attack. Word was passed along that the army would stop here and make camp. To protect their safety as much as possible, the trumpets were not blown, and, although it was quite cold, no fires were lit.

Arthur suddenly appeared from the congregation, and came over to where Amor and I were standing, saying under his kerchief that he had been looking for us.

'Margaret and I have decided that I should go tonight to investigate the fate of Grace's corporeal part. We fear that the weather and terrain will grow even more difficult in the coming days, and it might be harder for me to make this errand at a later date. If the going is tough, Margaret and I will need each other's support.

'I will slip there and back, remaining synchronous with Margaret, meaning that the time I pass when I am away will be the same as

38

passes for you. As a result, I will rejoin you down the road, when this march has progressed further.'

'Oh, Arthur, I am so relieved, and so grateful, I don't know what to say.' Tears welled up in my eyes.

'I have a vague sense that our meeting is more than coincidence,' Arthur said, 'but I do not know in what respect. Regardless, tell me what you can, Grace.'

'You mean about streets and things?' I asked.

'Yes,' Arthur replied. 'I expect to be taking the public bus to your home.'

I somehow imagined that he would be flying around the city like Superman.

'Of course,' I said. 'I live in Edmonton, in northern Alberta.'

'I know the city of Edmonton,' he said. 'There I will be speaking English!' Up to now we had been speaking Greek, though I was no longer consciously aware of it. My private thoughts, when formed in words, were English. I wondered how many languages Arthur had mastered in his travels.

'The district is Crestwood, on the north side, to the west along the river. You take the 14 bus south along 142nd Street, and get off at 96th Avenue. Is this what you want to know?'

I couldn't help that it seemed silly to me, a wraith in ancient Greece with red eyes and a black cloak telling a muscular hoplite the particulars of modern Edmonton trolley busses.

'Oh,' I said, 'the time was, or is, 1962. The third week of January, the 20th, I think, when I last remember. When you get off the bus at 96th Avenue, you are at a little shopping plaza. There is a Texaco at one end, and the Safeway at the other. On the next block, kitty-corner to the plaza, there is a curling rink, surrounded on its far sides by a park and community centre, including two ice rinks, and a small cinder block building used for dance classes and things.'

'Yes,' Arthur said, bringing significant concentration to bear. I was pleased and flattered.

'My house is at 9510 143rd Street, across from the curling rink south of 96th Avenue. 9-5-1-0,' I said. 'My mother lives with me there, and I have a roommate, Faith. I teach grade two at Crestwood school, which is over opposite the park on the north side.'

I was getting flustered.

'This will be clear when you get there.'

'That's fine, Grace,' Arthur replied. 'Where were you last?'

'Oh my, I do not know, Arthur. Not far from home, I know that. But I do not know exactly.'

In the morning Margaret said that Arthur had gone. The soldiers were getting themselves up, and those I could see looked somewhat melancholic. They had slept fully attired in the snow, with no fires. I gathered that it had, at least, been a mild night.

They ate some cold meat and started on their way. No ointment today, I thought. To my eye, the mountains opened to an even more austere country than the plain before them, where I had first arrived. I overheard one of the Greeks refer to this new landscape as 'desert,' which I thought was quite appropriate. It was snowy, but there was hard ground to walk on. As you often see on the Canadian prairie in winter, the land was blown clean, the snow gathering in periodic ridges and drifts. Good thing they weren't too fussy about where they relieved themselves.

'We will be two or three days crossing this ground,' Margaret observed as we walked. She was on the flank of her unit of slingers, and Amor and I walked alongside her, unseen. That was just about all that was said between us the whole day.

Which was curious, I thought, as I had been so full of questions, for which it seemed there was not enough time in the world to find answers! Now that I had the time and opportunity, those questions seemed less important. It may have been the sedate mood that day. I wondered what Amor thought about, walking along for hours and hours like this.

I decided I would ask him another time.

Now that I had made some tangible progress, with Arthur going to Edmonton, I was not *as* worried about my fate. It ran through my mind that he may not have any success. But, well, so be it then, I said to myself. I could not imagine having any better hands making the effort. No better hands in the world. He was strong, smart, honest, and politely spoken. A saint, I thought.

Now that we were friends, I felt sorry for Margaret, out there in the cold, while Amor and I were not affected. I never quite adjusted to it — walking right beside someone that I cared about, knowing

I was in one condition, more fortunate, and they were in another, less fortunate. It's hard to explain. It was not the same as visiting someone at their sick-bed, say, or passing a tramp on the street. Regardless, even if this experience did turn out to be more dangerous than expected, they *were* doing what they were doing by choice. I had not done anything in my life as menacing as this was for them, but I had put myself in challenging situations, and felt enriched by the ordeal. Once, for example, I went with three others down the North Saskatchewan River on a raft, from Rocky Mountain House to Edmonton. We worked hard along the way, but it was a beautiful time. What a nice thing to come to mind now! I thought. Another time I went hiking in the *winter* in Kananaskis, in the Rockies. That was harder. I was just a teenager.

Well, I've only just turned twenty-four, I thought, so I guess it wasn't really that long ago! But it did *seem* like a long time ago. I wondered if it was true that the days go by faster as you get older.

Most of the soldiers walked in silence, bringing their resolve exclusively to their long march. They kept themselves and their pack animals moving, I believed, by sheer force of will.

M argaret's estimate was close to the truth. In the afternoon of the third day the army reached the Euphrates. Here, north of the source of the Tigris, its course is to the southwest. Further along it jogs and bends to the south, then southeast, flowing down through Persia roughly parallel to the Tigris, to the west.

The army was at a spot not far from the Euphrates' headwater, and the river was only waist deep. That made for an easy crossing, for man and beast alike; but the water must have been *cold*, and I marvelled again at how durable these warriors were. Right through ice cold water, back into the wind and snow, and on their way.

For three days they had marched across the desert in silence, before this river crossing, without seeing a soul. And they marched another three days after the crossing, again alone and silent. Better alone than fighting, I thought, in this harsh weather. I imagined that *anyone* they might encounter would be hostile, until they arrived at the Greek towns on the Black Sea.

The terrain was level, with more and more trees about them as the hours passed — and more and more snow. On the third day a terrible wind came up. I was very unhappy to see them suffering as they were.

'Is there nothing we can do, Amor?' I said.

'No, I regret there is not,' Amor replied, 'though I fully share your compassion for their worsening condition.'

The wind whipped ice pellets into their faces, drove snow in their tunics, and numbed their bodies. The snow was knee deep, sometimes more, and I felt sure that many would suffer from frostbite. They had wrapped themselves fully with their robes, but this was far from adequate. Every step was strained, and progress was slow.

Through this phase, Xenophon was at the rear of the procession. Amor and I dropped back to see what, if anything, he had in mind to relieve the suffering.

He had already called his advisors, as it happened, and we arrived to find them declaring a resolution. They would slaughter an ox to appease the God compelling the wind.

'Do you have anything to do with this?' I asked Amor.

'Sacrifice they perform independent of my talent,' he replied.

'Does it *do* anything?'

'We shall observe the result momently, and decide.'

The wretched beast was just about finished anyway, but with appropriate ceremony its blood was spilled in offering. And within a few minutes, the wind subsided!

'There may be a benevolent spirit after all,' Amor said.

Word went up the column that the wind had let up because the Gods were pleased with the sacrifice, and with the piety of the sage that had made it.

'Well, that's good news for that guy's job,' I said, trying to be funny, but not meaning to be sarcastic.

'And for the men,' Amor replied, courteously disregarding my awkward wit. 'I was growing fearful they would fall in a spent heap in that torrent.'

Ahead the land grew more heavily wooded, with deeper and deeper snow. The trees must act as collectors, I thought, of what was blown up from the flat land to the south. I had never seen anything quite like it.

Xenophon had moved to the front, and was alternating groups of men to plough through the soft white wall ahead. I could see that, for the first time, there were casualties from exposure. The first to fall were slaves, being the poorest dressed, and poorest fed, but some soldiers were going too. The baggage train was particularly slow through the deep snow, and some of the beasts had also fallen dead.

Also for the first time, I saw other creatures on our side — these same succumbing to exposure on the march! I was startled at first, although I knew straight away what was happening. They would appear suddenly, a soft fuzz in empty space, coming to a sharp focussed form in a second or two — some running in futile flight, some standing paralyzed, others gazing around with outstretched arms — all in black, with the slight silvery sheen I had seen around my hands when I first arrived. And then they would be gone. It broke my heart to see it.

'Do not be unnerved by this spectacle, Grace,' Amor said, seeing me become a little dazed, 'however tragic you feel it to be.'

'Why do they come through here like this, Amor?'

'Death by exposure is, for many, a slow death,' Amor replied. 'They pass here when their lives are spent, but the blood of their substance is warm a little longer yet. Most have not had the necessary imagination to call elsewhere in time or space as they transit the boundary. Do not expect any report from them, Grace, as their minds are confused, numbed, or panicked.'

'It *is* upsetting, Amor.'

'Death is not usually rumoured for splendour,' Amor said, 'and this world where you now dwell is related to death as the womb is related to life. Here you cannot spend yourself in mourning. Hold your compassion in high esteem, and do not harden your heart against these influences. But also inform your heart that what you observe is natural and inevitable for all creatures, and this is where they will sometimes pass; while *no* new life, the seed of joys and hopes, will *ever* pass here.'

'Do you feel hope, Amor?'

'That question is complex,' Amor replied, 'and my full opinion cannot be expressed in a sentence. Regardless, hope is related to new life, to birth, even to sexuality. None of those things exist here.'

Xenophon called the march to a halt, and a camp was established at the head of the column. There was plenty of wood, and six large fires were built. The heat must have been fabulous, as the snow, drifted to five and six foot depths, melted away in huge spheres around the fires.

A strange conflict arose as the baggage train finally arrived at the campsite. The men who had made and tended the fires refused to let the baggage handlers warm themselves, except, as they put it, if they were supplied food to 'reward their work.' I heard one of the men refer to it as an exchange, of what one had for what the other had. I thought, in fact, they were all gone a little crazy from the strain.

In the course of that strain, I had lost track of Margaret. I was slightly alarmed when I realized this, and asked Amor if he knew where she was.

'When we dropped back and witnessed Xenophon host the sacrifice, Margaret carried on ahead, and I do not know her where-abouts. Let us presently search in earnest, with the army now collected in one place.'

Out of anxiety, I think, we began with the dead. About thirty corpses had been carried to the camp, many of whom Amor and I had seen pass by, over the boundary, earlier. They were laid to rest in the wood. Fortunately, Margaret was not among them. We thought to check each hand for the memento that Arthur and Margaret were looking for — a bit of a grizzly task. Several of the dead had worn rings, but we could find none with Hebrew writing on the face.

We went to each fire in turn, searching among the living, but could not see her. There were many, many men, mind you. We hoped she would be on the lookout for us. When I was riding on Amor's back, we together towered over everyone, and I thought we should be relatively easy for her to spot.

'Where *are* you, Margaret,' I said out loud in frustration.

'I am here,' I heard her say.

Amor turned like a shot, almost toppling me off, and we saw her. Dressed in black, with red eyes.

'Oh my God, oh my,' I said, 'are you dead? No, of course not! Not here. But what has happened?'

'I have fallen in the cold and snow, and lost consciousness,' Margaret said. 'I don't think I am seriously injured. I need only to be warmed, and I believe I will promptly revive. But that will have to proceed quickly. Still, it is interesting to know this existence, this sensation, wholly for the first time.'

Amor was silent, dumbstruck.

'Oh my,' I said. 'We're the Three Stooges on the Styx now.'

There was very little time to find Margaret's real self and revive her. As a candid measure of the urgency, however, we all just stood there, awkward and perplexed.

'What music do you hear?' I said to Margaret, eager to relieve the tension.

'I hear a chorus of many voices — strains associated with a twentieth-century composer, as yours are, but from an earlier decade — and these are not the echoes of the composer's work. They are, I think, the harmonies that he also *originally* heard, which he in turn captured in song — the very distinctive and stirring waves, ebbs, and torrential crests of *Carmina Burana*. I must have some old memory of the Huns.'

Amor appreciated my intent with the question, but also got us moving.

'There are none fallen at camp, Margaret was among the forward party, and has only lately broken over the boundary. I believe she must lie not far from here. Did you keep to the main path, Margaret, or did you stray on another errand?'

'I marched on the left flank against the wood with the main party,' she said. 'I broke only to check the hands of men that failed in the cold, making to assist, but it had been at least a quarter-hour since any such incident when I collapsed.'

'We will retrace that line, back from where the pack animals are now huddled. You must be patient and wait here,' Amor said to Margaret. 'It would not be propitious for you to come, should you discover your own flesh in a distraught condition.'

The moon was not bright, but we had sufficient light to make a competent search. We walked slowly back along the roadway. The path was well trampled in a broad swath, with steep walls of snow and trees to either side. It looked like a big tunnel.

We had only gone about a hundred yards when I saw something; though I could not know at first if it was her.

'Look there, Amor!' I said, pointing to an irregular hole in the white bulwark to our right. We quickly made our way over, and saw that it was Margaret. It looked like she had just dropped, from cold and fatigue.

'I wish Arthur were here,' I said, feeling guilty he was away on my behalf. 'If Arthur were here this would not have happened.'

'Never mind, Grace,' Amor said reassuringly. 'Our task now is to relieve the situation.'

'What can we do, Amor?' We both knew that we were about as useful in the real world as viewers to distressed actors in a TV show.

'There is a link between ourselves and the travellers,' Amor said, 'as you observed taking your reflexion in Arthur's shield.'

He stood still for a minute, thinking.

'We may be able to take advantage of that same phenomena,' Amor said, 'to draw attention to our fallen soldier.'

We went back to the baggage camp, where some men who had eaten and warmed themselves were attending to the animals, as best they could, by torchlight.

'Let us see if that benevolent spirit casts us a fortunate shadow now. Margaret's shield remains in the grip of her hand, inclined toward the path. We need to cast a reflexion — you will observe my plan.'

We waited until a group of three soldiers had, in making their rounds, come to the extreme rear, on the side of the road where Margaret lay. I jumped down off Amor's back, and returned part way back down the road toward her.

The fortunate moment came, when Amor could get between the beasts and their attendants, facing down toward Margaret and me. The men had paused to rest for a moment, and relaxed their torches at chest height.

The torches carried a large light — large enough that Amor could pretty much put his whole head in the flame.

Which is exactly what he did. He put his face in the fire.

And, I must confess, it was quite a sight! The blaze flared up in an exaggerated outline of his features, sketched in dazzling crimson, bright yellow, and blue — a striking, eerie spectre in flame.

Amor was untouched himself, but the ever-wary Greeks reacted as hoped, paralyzed with shock for a second, and then running away — in Margaret's direction, as Amor had intended. The transformed torch had been quickly dropped, but the other two men ran carrying theirs with them.

I ran ahead of them, having given myself a head start. Coming to Margaret's body, I knelt beside her. I waved one of my sleeves in front of her shield, hoping to add some sparkle or glimmer to the torchlight. I didn't know how far this connexion we had with the travellers' things might go, but anything was worth a try.

Whether or not I had any effect, one of the men saw the reflexion of his torch from the shield. His mind already being focussed on the paranormal, he interpreted this as a sign.

'There is something here! The phantoms have startled us to discovery!' he brusquely shouted to his colleagues.

I marvelled at that for a second. It was a statement of fact.

'Good plan, Amor!' I said, my arm around his neck, as we watched them carry her away to the campfire. When Amor and I got back to the spot from which we had departed, she was gone. I had prayed she would be gone, back to life.

In the morning, Amor and I saw Margaret was warmed and rested, and we positioned ourselves to walk nearby her when the march resumed.

It had been hard going for the army the day before; but, for many at least, it would be fair to say they hadn't seen anything yet.

It was bitterly cold, Margaret reported, though the sun was bright. Nobody had found much to eat.

Amor wished to stay with Xenophon, so we joined the rear guard, where the Commander had stationed himself. No one seemed concerned that Margaret had broken from her usual company.

We began coming up on men that had fallen in the snow. Someone reported to Xenophon that they suffered from 'bulimia.' He said he had no idea what this meant, and was informed that if they had something to eat they could continue the march.

I was impressed by Xenophon's energy and devotion. He personally made his way up to the baggage animals, and rooted around for food. He called orders to some servants, who were still in good condition, to run what he had found to the collapsed men. With just a little in their stomachs they were able to move along again.

The light-armoured peltasts in the front were starting to move along much faster, as they had when we marched to the mountains for battle, and were soon well ahead of the hoplites and baggage.

Chirisophus, the general who was given charge of the forward group, had an easier time of it that night than Xenophon and his party, much farther behind. Chirisophus and his men made it to a walled group of villages, where they encountered some women taking water from a well. They were Persian, and Chirisophus told them through a translator that he and his men were going from the King to the satrap. The women replied that the satrap was not there, but invited them through the ramparts, where Chirisophus met with their leader. He was given permission to camp at the town with his men, within the shelter of the walls.

We only heard about this a little later. The situation was quite different back with Xenophon and the slower-moving contingent. They were, more or less, falling to pieces.

They spent the night with no fires, and virtually no food. Many soldiers died where they slept. I noticed a few drift over the boundary before going. Most, apparently, just died.

I came face to face suddenly with one who passed over briefly. I started to speak to him, but he seemed stunned with fear — believing, I think, that he was in the presence of a sorceress of the underworld.

Others among the living were suffering the loss of fingers and toes, and others yet were blind from the bright sun on the snow. The chances of them surviving, I thought, were just about zero. It was hard enough for the able-bodied to keep going.

To make matters worse, some Persian thugs had gathered themselves into a militia, and were attacking our rear. They were also capturing baggage animals that fell behind — although, being bandits, they could be heard quarrelling violently over the spoils.

As the march resumed, more and more Greeks were dropping, saying they could go no further. Xenophon appealed to them, as many as he could, trying to get them up, prodding them, telling them the enemy had raised an army and were upon them.

I saw that Xenophon's own feet were wrapped in undressed ox-hide, tied around with cords. While, fortunately, he appeared to be in stable health, he looked like one of those supremely tragic prisoners-of-war you would see in the newsreels, plodding down a winter road somewhere in eastern Europe, with their feet bundled like sacks of potatoes.

He was very persuasive, but persuasion was not adequate, and he became angry. The men responded, asking him to kill them. I heard Xenophon say, 'This would indeed be the best course, to strike terror in the advancing enemy'; but he delayed the order.

Instead, he called for all fit hands in the column to come to the rear, ready for battle. Several hundred came — I was ever amazed at their rugged courage — and were ordered into ranks.

And they attacked, with great shouts! Not only from those pursuing the enemy with spears. The sick and injured back with us, others lying on the ground — everyone was shouting and banging sticks on shields, whatever was at hand.

'The enemy was struck with alarm,' Xenophon announced on his return, and had fled.

Xenophon visited those who were sick and couldn't travel. He told them he would send men back to collect them the next day, when, hopefully, the army would have found shelter and food.

There was more trouble further along, with the hoplites that had carried on ahead while Xenophon dealt with the bandits. We caught up to them, and found men in the snow — *covered* with snow, not having moved for hours!

Xenophon called for a messenger, to find out what the problem was. The servant reported that the whole army had stopped there to rest, that they could go no further that day.

The next morning, after another night with no fires and no food, Xenophon again was as good as his word, sending some young people, who were still fit, back to assist the sick and wounded. The rest resumed the march north. It was better going than it had been the day before, as the weather was milder, and the forward party, under Chirisophus, had cut through the snow and beaten a path. But the hoplites and supply caravan still hadn't eaten or had any proper chance to refresh themselves, so it remained a morbid procession. I did not see anyone fall dead as we went, at least.

I was becoming anxious about Arthur. Not so much worrying about his success on my behalf, but concerned because he left just before the worst of it for the Greeks, which was exactly what he wished to avoid. When he comes back, things will probably be easier again, and he will feel badly about his timing. I was afraid that he would hold some resentment toward me as the cause of all the bother in the first place.

'Oh well,' I said aloud, 'as long as Margaret is healthy when he returns.' And the rest of us. I was beginning to feel a little tired from time to time.

I asked Amor what I might do to perk myself up.

'This would suggest that your fate is in the world of men, and that you have not been cast across the boundary to wander indefinitely,' he said. 'Your available time is plentiful yet, but let us hope that Arthur has success, or that your material part will soon be restored in some other way. If not, you will come to crisis.'

I appreciated his being candid, and I was careful not to get excited or show any despair in return. I *was* despairing, however, as I didn't know what to do. For now, I thought, I guess there isn't anything I *can* do but be patient and wait for Arthur.

Within a few hours, some of Xenophon's emissaries were returning with the sick and injured. Some were hobbling along together, where the disabled could walk with assistance; others who could not walk were being carried on makeshift stretchers, fashioned from saplings.

Then there was something of a commotion. A company of warriors that had been with Chirisophus came back down the road to see what had become of the rest in the rear. Word quickly spread that the peltasts were camped at a village — where there was food to be had — just two miles distant. The general mood among the hoplites brightened immediately.

The men that had come back down from the village were already fed, and were better rested than those still on the trail, so they took over the transportation of the sick and injured. Before too long the whole army was rejoined at the town.

Once within the ramparts, I said to Amor that this was the strangest city I had ever seen! The homes were all underground! There were actually several villages, over a large area. The houses were entered by ladder, down a hole (like a well). This would have been awkward for Amor, except that there were other broad tunnels dug for animals — all of which they kept underground in their homes for the winter! There were cows, sheep, chickens, and goats, all raising a racket (and a sharp bouquet!), with supplies of feed stored there for them all.

Xenophon seemed to hit it off with the town leader. The Greek generals had drawn lots to see which hamlet they would occupy with their men. I wasn't clear what difference there might be between them, but thought this procedure must be in case there *were* any differences found after the fact. The choices would have been made by chance.

Xenophon invited the head man to have supper with him. When they were sitting together, Xenophon assured him through an interpreter that he need have no fear for the safety of his people, and further pledged that he would re-stock the food and drink they were consuming when he reached another tribe further down the road. Robbing Peter to pay Paul, I thought. I found it quite amusing, that way of thinking and that way of life, though only because it was a moral problem I was helpless to resolve.

To show him that he intended to co-operate, the mayor took Xenophon to where some wine was buried. It must have been pretty potent stuff, as it caused even these stout-hearted Greeks to gasp and choke at first. Many mixed it with water.

I was happy to see the soldiers able to shake off some of what they had suffered with strong drink.

They were still eating and making merry in the morning. Amor and I followed Xenophon as he went with the mayor to find Chirisophus. At each group of houses they passed, Xenophon looked in on his men. Each time it was the same thing — they welcomed him as their guardian, and insisted he sit and join them. It was heartwarming to see, really. At each table they had a variety of cooked meats and breads, together with the strong wine, which they sucked up from large bowls with straws. The bowls had barley floating on top, which I thought must be to keep the wine from spoiling. The head man declined to join in the festivities, unless he saw one of his relatives was present.

We saw Margaret at one of the houses. She was dozing, but I nudged her and asked if she was okay. I said that Amor and I were following Xenophon around from village to village. She said that

51

she was fine, and happy there was lots of food and time to sleep with no immediate threat.

After much chicken, pork, beef, vegetables, loaves, and wine at various abodes, our touring party came upon Chirisophus feasting with his men. They all had garlands of hay tied around their heads, and were being waited on by Armenian boys!

Xenophon and Chirisophus sat together with their host, the chief, and questioned him further. They learned that the country was Armenia, and that the next on their way was Chalybes. He gave them directions on how to get there from here.

The Armenians had a number of fine horses, and Xenophon went away from this meeting with several colts, which he distributed among his generals. He left a horse that had been taken from Tiribazus, in poor condition after the recent ordeal, telling the mayor to fatten it up and sacrifice it. Amor could not restrain a little tremor in his coat at the shoulder, which I took as a wince.

'How oft the darkest hour of ill, Breaks brightest into dawn,' I thought, quoting Euripides (who was probably first writing those lines the same instant I said them there!), marvelling at the army's rapid transformation. One day cold, starving, desperate, and falling dead. The next day, warm, well fed, and living it up. They weren't home yet, of course. And those who did make it home safely would soon be off somewhere else fighting again.

That was just their way of life, I thought. As long as there was sufficient rest and reward punctuating the hardship, it was counted a good life.

Probably little different from us in the 1960s, really, I thought. The highs and lows here were just a little more bald.

Then, as the afternoon was drawing to a close, I finally heard Amor say what I had been longing to hear.

'Look, Grace! There is Arthur.'

I quickly jumped up on Amor's back, and we rode over to him at a brisk gait.

'Arthur! Arthur!' I called, 'We are so *glad* to see you!'

'Hello Grace! Hello Amor!' Arthur called in return, unconcerned about being overheard. I don't think there was anyone in earshot anyway. In the cold weather, the locals only seemed to come out to get water from the well at the gate, and for their toilet. The Greeks were, strictly speaking, camping outdoors, but most seemed to have found themselves a spot in one of the many homes, where it was warmer. Now at midmorning, most were sleeping off the long night of eating and drinking.

Which is what Amor was telling Arthur.

'Is Margaret well?' Arthur asked.

'Yes, Margaret is well,' Amor said. 'She is sleeping now, in the stables adjoining the dwelling six doors down' — and he gently shook his nose upwards, gesturing in the direction of the house. 'You may already have been informed, Arthur, that the Greeks passed two days plagued with inclement weather, and bandits.'

'I'm so sorry Arthur!' I blurted out. 'I have been worried that you would be upset, because you went away just when things became quite difficult, which is exactly —'

'Grace, Grace,' Arthur said, interrupting, 'please be calm, and rest easy. This army has endured many hardships, and I knew there was no predicting what may happen. As long as all is well now.'

'Thanks, Arthur,' I added softly, 'all *is* well now.'

'I have had a very interesting time. Very, very interesting. I am not sure where to begin, and moreover have learned some things that I am not altogether sure how to tell you.'

'Bad things?' I asked.

'No, not bad things!' Arthur said. 'Not at all.'

'Perhaps you would prefer to rest, and spend some time with Margaret, before telling us what you have learned on your journey,' Amor said.

'Well, yes, I would — but I know that Grace must be very eager to hear the story,' Arthur replied.

'Yes, I am,' I said. 'Can you just tell me now if I'm okay?'

'You've had a serious injury — knocked by a moving car, you fell hard to the ice in the curling rink parking lot, across the street from your house. Your skull was fractured, suffering a severe concussion, and you are now comatose. Your body is failing, and needs you back. That is, it needs your propinquity there to stimulate blood flow and the like, to encourage your own recovery. Your body will not call you there, however, as your starved brain is presently insensitive to this need.'

'Something of a paradox,' Amor said.

'Yes,' Arthur responded, 'not a hopeless one by any means, but the necessary means are not known to me yet.'

M argaret and Arthur talked over a hearty lunch at the house. Amor and I left them be, naturally. The rhythms of the music had become more agitated — no, more *aggressive*. Still the unmistakable colour of Meat Loaf's voice, but a harder sound.

You need somebody you can hold onto.

I thought I must be repressing some bigger desperation.

You never can be too sure about the girl.

'This might be a very pleasant time, here in the nether world,' I said to Amor, 'if I weren't always worried, or full of questions — or now, also full of curiosity about what else exactly Arthur has discovered.'

'You will go away with a wealth of new knowledge and experience, Grace,' he replied, 'about other lands and times, about this place, and the music.'

'And especially about you, Amor,' I said with sincerity.

'Thank you, Grace.'

Three days passed before I learned anything more from Arthur. He told me at one point that he needed to consider things for a while, and that I would understand fully when I knew the story.

I believed that he was telling me the truth. Not only because I knew he was trustworthy, but I could *see* he was having trouble working out some part of it. There was a particular quality to the way he spoke, which you only see in people who are completely kind, devoted to doing the right thing — and in distress.

I thought that having a knowledge of the past and the future must bring with it any number of moral burdens, which others did not face. Not that they — Arthur and Margaret, as travellers — considered themselves to be any different than anyone else, or to be invested with any special privileges.

It was simpler than that. Not unlike Christmas, I thought. The whole family might know what is in a package addressed to you, but they will not tell you. They know your future! But it would not be *right* to tell you about it before you made the discovery for yourself at the proper time, on Christmas morning.

Still, trusting in others this way took a lot of patience. I could see, as well, that my energy was running down a little each day. Only a little, but enough that I could notice.

'Are my eyes less bright now?' I said to Arthur, meeting up with him one afternoon. We had been five days in the underground town by that time.

'Yes, I see that your vitality is declining. But I would also say that you have a good amount of time left.'

He paused, as though working up his resolve.

'Here, let me find Margaret, and I will tell you more of the story I have for you now.'

While we waited for Arthur to get Margaret, I told Amor that I wished now I could just stay there with him.

'Everyone connected with this world is so kind and trustworthy,' I said. 'For all my worry about getting back home, and about dying, I feel safe here. None of the trouble of the real world touches us.'

'Those tied to this sphere *are* kind, it is true,' Amor responded. 'I have observed that only those with a considerate heart will *find* their composure here, whether their stay be fleeting or lengthy. The base cause underlying this fact, however, is that there is nothing to be gained on this side. There is no intrigue that would bear any profit, as there is simply nothing to be had.'

'Then is there no evil here, Amor?'

He had to think about that.

'You may ask why, even with nothing to gain, the experience of this world does not involve the tensions that put men against each other — of contempt, or jealousy, or other hostility. Your mind forms its thoughts here as before, and is as equally *capable* of anger as benevolence. I cannot tell you as any objective fact, but I have observed that egregious behaviour is shed by those who possess themselves here. In the world of men, the value of one's personality and character — the whole of one's true possession — is both driven and obscured by external pressures, needs, and desires. Those influences do not exist in this world, so the motive impulses of good and evil which you ask about simply do not have the same dominion. But — remember this also means that our life in the twilight is largely benign.'

55

'Except for the odd haunting, and bullying dead sheep and oxen.'

Amor wheezed at that. Another laugh, I thought, and I laughed too. I realized at that moment that I loved him. My friend. My good friend.

Arthur returned with Margaret to find us still smirking, though he did not seem to notice. They were also in good spirits.

'This rest has been healthy for everyone,' Arthur said, 'though the march will have to be resumed soon.'

He invited us to sit down. We did so, although I think Amor was more comfortable standing.

'It was distressing for me to see you injured, Grace,' Arthur said, 'as I'm sure you can appreciate. I arrived in Edmonton only hours before the incident, as it turned out, slipping in at a major intersection a short way up from your neighbourhood, north on 142nd Street. I begged bus fare from a passer-by, after stealing a suit of clothes and topcoat from a tailor's shop on the boulevard.

'By the way,' he added, 'before slipping back I returned the suit and coat, and left money at the shop. Unfortunately, one has to be somewhat mercenary from time to time on first arriving at a new place. Please don't imagine I consider these actions to be in any way commendable. Especially as the money I left for the suit was yours, Grace, taken without your consent.

'I got off the bus at the Crestwood Plaza, as you advised. It was 6:00 p.m., and the stores were closing. Being the dead of winter, it had already been dark for over an hour — and was, I think, *rather* colder in Edmonton than it has been for these Greeks at the worst of their distress! I walked down 96th Avenue, first along the length of the plaza parking lot; then down alongside some homes across from the curling rink; then followed the length of the fence bordering the school-ground, across from the public park. Next I walked down the street adjacent to the park on its west side, and continued along as it curves around to join the avenue on the east side, where I approached your house.

'I was at the corner when I saw a woman leave your house. The number on the post in the front garden was clear at that distance. She walked briskly across the street, not yet adjusted to the cold. I could not know if it was you, your mother, or your roommate

Faith, and did not know if the unknown trauma had happened yet.
'I had not long to wait. I was shocked to see you struck, then, virtually in front of my eyes! A motorist lost control on the ice, accelerating out of a parking spot. It was a big heavy car — a Pontiac with a straight-eight, I noticed — and difficult to stop. You were facing away from each other as he came out. You were walking — and then, thump! down you went.

'I ran like blazes, and it was only a matter of seconds before I was upon you. I could see that you very badly hurt, bleeding from the head. The motorist was *horrified* at what he had done, and quickly pulled blankets from the back seat of the car. We rolled you over onto them, ever so gently, and covered you up snugly. I said I was going for assistance. I ran to your house and rang the bell, calling for help. Faith opened the door.

' "Faith! Faith!" I cried, "Grace has had a serious accident. We must call an ambulance." She told me to come in, and went and dialled the phone. After informing the operator of the emergency, she rushed back and put on her coat and hat.

' "Where did you get those shoes?!" she said, pointing to my ox-hide foot-wrap. The fact was I could not find new shoes when I borrowed the other clothes, but I told Faith that my shoes and money had been stolen. An improbable story, but I did not feel I should explain the truth. She pulled some rubber snow-boots with woolly insides out from the closet, and told me to put them on.

'We ran back across the street. A dozen-odd people had gathered, and the police had arrived. I introduced us to the officer as close friends of the victim, and told him we had ordered an ambulance. When Faith saw you, Grace, she burst into tears, weeping almost uncontrollably.

'The ambulance arrived in just a few minutes, and I escorted Faith back to the house. She invited me in, and poured hot coffee from an already-percolated pot. Once we both were better composed, after the shock, I said that I was an old friend of yours, on my way to visit you when I witnessed the accident. I repeated that my money had been stolen, regretting the lie, and that I had nowhere to stay. Faith, believing I spoke the truth — which I did in every other way but about the theft — and having witnessed my caring and concern for you, said I could stay in the guest room.

'The next day, Faith drove us to the hospital in your car to see you. She said your mother was away for the weekend, visiting her friends Tom and Sylvia in Lloydminster, about two hours away by car in the winter. At first, the nurse would not allow us into the ward, saying that visits were restricted to members of the immediate family. We appealed, however, saying that Faith was your roommate, and I an old friend, that your mother was away, and how we would be quite ashamed if your mother returned and we had not seen you. At length the nurse consented, and led us to a large examination room, where we waited for the doctor.

'There was a man there, with his son, who explained that the boy was in for a blood test. Courteously passing the time, he said that when they passed the gift kiosk in the hospital lobby, the child had asked how the blind man operating it could tell if people had stolen something, and how he knew the price of the merchandise.

'"A lively, enquiring mind," I replied, just as the doctor called us into your room. I was very unhappy to see you there, unconscious, with various life-support devices attached.

'The doctor explained that you had suffered a fractured skull, and were comatose. He said that there was no way of knowing when, or if, you would wake up. Faith was deeply shaken when the doctor suggested that you may not wake, and I put my arm around her, to offer comfort. She is very devoted to you, Grace.'

'Yes, we are close friends,' I said, trembling.

'We stayed for about thirty minutes. Faith sat holding your hand, speaking to you. She said that she believed you could probably hear her, even if you could not respond. I knew that, for you, this was not the case; but was touched regardless, and said nothing.

'I have postponed telling you these facts, in part, Grace, knowing that it would be difficult for you. These have been the main details of your injury, and I see now that you are agitated, so permit me to delay the rest of the story, such as it is, until tomorrow.'

The happy mood we began with *had* declined somewhat as the story progressed, certainly; but I was not shocked or gloomy, and told him so. I also thanked him for being frank and direct about it. And for caring for me there, and for the help and support he had given to Faith.

It was good to know what had happened, but it didn't shed any light on what to do about it.

He did not resume the story the next day, as the two of them were busy with the rest making preparations to leave. We had been staying at the underground village for seven days by that time, and were planning to depart the next morning.

Xenophon told the village chief that he was coming with the army as a guide. Although it was not a request, the man obliged, and went to collect his things. He was placed in the charge of Chirisophus. The man also brought one of his sons along, who was given to the care of someone called Plisthenes of Amphipolus.

After three days' march, there was a row between Chirisophus and Xenophon. Apparently Chirisophus, who was again leading the forward party while Xenophon took up the rear, grew angry with the guide for not leading them to any villages. The mayor protested that there were none to be found in this part of the country, but Chirisophus beat him regardless. He escaped during the night, leaving his son behind.

Xenophon was not pleased with any of this, finding Chirisophus at fault both for punishing the man, and then failing to guard him properly.

The chill between them lasted for several days, though the army kept on marching without incident, making about fifteen miles a day. After a week they came to a river crossing, which Xenophon thought must be the Phasis, but which Arthur said he knew was the Araxes. It was of no real consequence, so Arthur said nothing.

Xenophon ordered the army to a brisker pace after the crossing, and over the following two days we made about sixty miles. On the second day, in the morning, Arthur told me more about his trip.

'I did little else of any importance while I was in Edmonton, Grace, though it was an interesting visit,' he started saying at one point as we walked alone together. 'Faith renewed her invitation to be a guest at your home, and the next day your mother returned.'

He paused for several minutes.

'She was shocked and upset, naturally. The three of us went together to the hospital that afternoon. We found you unchanged, except as the doctor said you were tending to grow weaker rather than stronger.'

I was feeling ever weaker as the days passed now, here on the other side, though I did not tell Arthur that. He could probably see it in my eyes.

'Grace, there is something else,' he continued. 'I have not known if I should tell you, or how to tell you. I think now that you should know.'

A minute or so passed as he collected his thoughts.

'You must not be confused about one thing, Grace, which I have told you before, but will say again. Our lives as travellers run in a straight line day-to-day, the same as anyone else — except that we can move in time and place, whereas others can relocate only in place. Because there are so few of us, and because we have travelled in regular ways, odd things generally do *not* occur.'

'What are you getting at?' I asked gently.

'An odd thing has occurred,' he replied.

'What?' I said.

'That was perhaps the wrong way to preface what I have to say. Please allow me to first tell you the fact which has caused me this awkwardness.'

I was all ears.

'Margaret is your mother. Or she will be in the future, after we have had another eleven years of life and travel in various other times and places, and then two years of settled living in England. When you were traumatized, you needed help urgently. Without knowing it, you — your subconscious, if you like — sought out your mother. Here.'

To say I was stunned would be an understatement — but I was not unhappy! I *thought* she had looked familiar when we first met, although she would be about thirty-seven years younger now. People change a great deal over that length of time, of course.

'What was odd was *my* meeting her there in the future,' Arthur said. 'I recognized her immediately, although she was much older, and she me. We both gasped! Fortunately Faith was not at home then. After telling her about your accident, and taking time for her to convalesce from the shock, she explained to me that we had travelled together for several years after Xenophon, but there came a time when she wanted to stop and settle down. She was then thirty-three years old. We had come to England, in 1936. She met a man there, fell in love, and stayed. You came along in 1938.'

'My father was killed in World War II, though I was very close to his dad, my grandfather.'

'I know of your father,' Arthur replied, 'though Margaret — or, as you know her, Meg — would not tell me about anything else that had happened over the times between now and then. I did not *wish* to know. But seeing her there was strange for me. She was already fifty-nine, and knew the full history of our adventures together over the years! Strange.'

'Yes,' I said. 'I'm glad you also find that strange!'

'Of course, I now know this important information about her future, which she must not discover. Do you understand? You must not say anything to her about this, however difficult that might be. She has many years ahead to live, in a number of different times and places, before becoming your mother. Like me, I *promise* she would prefer not to know what is going to happen.'

'Knowing what is going to happen, you might change it,' I said without thinking. I already knew better than that.

'What you say is ambiguous, Grace — it *will* happen as it has, or does. It remains, however, that these are the very kind of mind-tangling situations we scrupulously avoid. There is usually nothing *to* avoid! This was an uncanny accident — except that it was not an accident, in that you came here to *find* her.'

'I understand,' I said.

'But Margaret must not know.'

'I understand.'

'There is one more thing, which you might find interesting to learn. Margaret knows *now*, here with the Greeks, that I went ahead in time to help you. When I saw her in Edmonton, she still remembered my mercy trip. She could not recall *where* I had gone, however. She said that many years had passed, and many adventures, and she had forgotten. As well, she was numb with cold and fatigue at the time, she said, and had quickly lost the details.'

'Yes, I understand. People usually forget things as time goes by, especially things that happen at a stressful time,' I said.

'She had not forgotten you, however. When she saw me there and I told her about the accident, she immediately made the connexion.

61

"*This* is what you slipped ahead for? To help *my* daughter? Oh my God," she said. "That wraith was *my* daughter! Oh my God." I replied that this was true, and that Grace must have swept through the ether in search of *her*, on some unconscious impulse.

'This was the twist, not unlike something you might find in an adventure story — in the future, in Edmonton, Margaret told me: "I was so taken with the wraith at the time, long ago, I named my daughter after her!" It is really neither here nor there, Grace, but you were named after yourself.'

We laughed, and I looked forward to telling Amor the story.

'Can I tell Amor?'

'Yes, you may,' Arthur said. 'He will know to keep silent.'

'Why is this *happening* to me?' I asked, feeling foolish after blurting it out.

'I cannot tell you that, exactly. I am moved to assist you solely out of compassion for your situation. It does happen, however, that I have learned your predicament is central to events affecting Margaret and me personally, in the future we first departed from.'

'But if those things happened for you, then they *will* happen!' I said, aware I was haplessly repeating the idea back to him without much conviction, and knowing he would not elaborate.

'We are, apparently, still responsible to work out the means.'

'It is all so *complex*, how things are interwoven. We're trying to make things work out, when we don't know the first thing about how the universe works, or what God is, or anything,' I said, exasperated. 'Does this mean we are all idiots, playing out a pre-determined script for things?'

'We just *live our lives*, Grace, and the future unfolds on its own. Whichever way around it might occur, an advance knowledge of what happens is, simply, an awareness of what chanced to unfold for the world. But because it *can* be complex, metaphysically, that knowledge is generally best not had. You can see now, I think, how little impact a true knowledge of future events has on the present — but, ironically, how *encumbering* any such knowledge can be. This is the folly of oracles and fortunes, and why travellers are so careful about the facts they acquire. And Amor also. That horse could fill in more than a few details for Mr. H.G. Wells' *Outline of History*, as well as *The Shape of Things to Come*!'

He smiled warmly, and we walked along in silence. I was reassured that I seemed to have a role in the future; although it occurred to me that the result of this 'predicament' could be anything, including my death.

I wondered where God was, the God that had spoken to Job. 'Elizabeth will tell you about Job, and the last time God was heard to speak,' Arthur said.

I blushed, as I had muttered my wondering out loud. I drifted back to the music.

Mr. Loaf was repeating, *Life is a lemon and I want my money back*.

I asked Amor if he had met H.G. Wells on this side. He said no, but he had seen other poets and philosophers from that era. Orwell had appeared once, he said, boastful of his gains from a meagre output. He felt depressed on some account, Amor said.

He added that he saw Cummings from time to time, usually making ontological arguments for his failure to gain appreciation in his own time. 'I thought we might see him in the mountains. He has often called himself an inspector of snowstorms.'

He also said Wittgenstein had stayed here, a wraith for some time before his death, but that 'the premature departure of his spirit went largely unnoticed by his peers.' I thought this must be a joke, and I laughed, to which Amor gave me a friendly, quizzical look.

Towards the end of the day the march was halted. We had come to within three miles of a mountain pass — the only available road — and Chirisophus's scouts had reported that it was held by packs of Chalybes, Taochi, and Phasians.

A meeting of the generals was called to decide on a strategy. It was a treat to witness the dialogue — the fullest expression of the importance of elegant rhetoric for the Greeks.

Speeches were given in turn by Chirisophus, Cleanor (a senior general), and Xenophon. Chirisophus mainly served to define the problem. Cleanor expanded on his observations, concluding that the army should attack. Xenophon expanded on both, offering them a lengthy, eloquent analysis of the issues, his wish to minimize their losses, and his proposed tactic. That tactic was to take the heights by stealth that night. He believed if the core position was taken in this way, their chances would be much better than if they took on a prepared enemy in a direct assault. As well, when the enemy saw that the heights were lost, they would be much more likely to disperse, feeling their cause was lost.

I thought that was clever, although it would probably only work in this restricted terrain. Instead of attacking the enemy army in the usual way, he would sneak in with a guerrilla force and take their base camp, to undermine their resistance.

They concluded with an unusual exchange, highlighting the longstanding pointed rivalry (and worse) between Athens and Sparta. Xenophon, an Athenian, said that this 'theft of the heights' would be simplicity itself for a Spartan, trained as children to steal. Chirisophus, a Spartan, replied that it was an equally natural activity for the Athenians, expert at stealing public funds, and electing their very *best* swindlers to serve in government.

'An oblique exchange of compliments,' Amor remarked.

Xenophon proposed that he personally lead a party of hoplites on the mission. Chirisophus objected, saying that if he went, the command of the rear guard would be left vacant. So three other men were chosen instead, one with a unit of hoplites, and two others with light-armoured infantry. They departed after the army had finished their evening meal, and were instructed to light fires as soon as they had possession of the heights.

Meanwhile, Chirisophus mobilized the main body of the army into batteries in a broad attack formation, as a diversion. They marched about a mile further toward the pass, making a good amount of noise. Had *I* been in the hills, I would have been fooled — believing I was in for a fight, head on, and investing my energy in making those preparations.

It turned out to be a combined effort. The advance party took the heights, as planned, but the enemy did not submit. It was a stand-off till morning, when the enemy engaged the advance party on the heights. Hearing the fighting, Chirisophus slaughtered a sheep in sacrifice, and ordered his troops to advance. The bulk of the enemy was guarding the pass. The Greeks were quickly gaining the advantage on the heights, however, and some of the enemy force was sent back to assist.

I was terrified knowing that both Arthur and Margaret were in the war party, now advancing to attack the enemy. I knew that they must survive — Margaret *will* become my mother, I thought — but that didn't mean they wouldn't suffer any amount of injury in the meantime. Chirisophus sent the peltasts, on the double, to attack the main force at the pass. The hoplites followed at quick march, with much whooping and hollering.

I was relieved when the engagement began to fizzle out. The Greeks on the heights were pummelling the foreigners, we heard, which took the spirit out of those defending the pass. They began to run away in larger and larger numbers, and the way was soon free. The Greeks were very good at this business of war, I thought, and they were resourceful and strong — as well as generally larger than the Armenians.

There was a celebration at the heights, with animal sacrifices. They put up a stone memorial, which the Greeks called a τρόπαιον, or trophy, a monument to victory in war.

While this was going on, Amor and I were inspecting the dead — which fortunately were not numerous — looking for the ring.

I don't know what it is but it just won't quit.

There is a real sublimity about a heldentenor, I thought. Something so rare.

And wherever you are and wherever you go there's always gonna be some light.

More and more often now I would suddenly find my head swimming, and I would feel deflated, tired, and despairing. All of the assurances I had had from Arthur, what else he had told me and had implied about my future — *the* future — seemed like a dream. A dream within a dream. Although I guess I had to believe the facts, they seemed empty. Empty hopes. A complex fantasy. I wondered more and more about God.

I remembered God saying to Isaiah, 'I form the light, and create darkness. I make peace, and create evil. I the Lord do all these things.' That statement was so *loaded*, I thought to myself, though I suppose it only has impact if you count the whole context as objective truth. The same way that people can only hurt you if you lend weight to their opinions.

'Though he slay me, yet I will trust in him,' I remembered Job saying. He may yet slay me now, I thought. Nothing of what Arthur had said to me really assured that my life might resume as it was. Amor could usually see when I was distressed.

'More and more, Amor, I find my mood suddenly swinging down,' I said to him at one point, when the army had stopped to gather supplies. The battle won, the men had advanced through the pass, and were taking food at a village on the other side.

'Your time grows critical, Grace. I pray that the necessary articles of deliverance will show themselves soon,' Amor said.

I couldn't squeeze out a single word in reply. I was so upset I could hardly contain myself. I remembered how I had been upset like this once before.

I had an abscess under the skin on my leg, which hæmorrhaged. The pain was terrific. Once it was removed, I was unable to walk for a few days. Normally my mother would have helped me at a time like that, but I was away at school then — the only time I've *really* been on my own. I was too shy to ask my new friends for help. The difficulty of pulling myself along the floor wore down my spirits — even as I reminded myself over and over that others suffered more acutely and much longer than this. I was only a couple of days recovering, after all. But, while it lasted, it took me half an hour to get to the bathroom, and I couldn't put a tin of soup on the stove. Pulling myself upright to get something out of the fridge caused blood to pour from the wound, which I had to re-dress myself three times each day.

At one point I remember wishing, wishing, wishing that someone — anyone — would come to the door and say, 'Hey! I'll bet *you* would like a nice cup of tea! Well, let me put the kettle on!'

And then I cried and cried.

Well, when that performance was done, I was still flat on the floor, still only half way to the bathroom. Nothing had changed. I just had to keep on going.

'I just have to keep on going,' I said.

Amor remarked he often saw Jung, and had spoken with him. 'The vastest intellect among men,' he said, 'his spirit moved freely here while he lived.' Once, he said, he asked him about God.

'Jung replied that he was writing an essay about the God of Job, the God that once spoke to man, who once knew man. He said that

66

"God can boast of his superior power and enact laws which mean less than air to him. Murder and manslaughter are mere bagatelles for him. He can play the grand seigneur and generously recompense his bondslave for the havoc. *So you have lost your sons and daughters? No harm done. I will give you new and better ones.* That is what I will write about the God of Job!" he said to me.'

'I have not seen very many others here,' I said, 'except for the dying Greek soldiers back in the cold and snow.'

'You have been on this side a short time, and we have been in remote parts of the land,' Amor replied. 'As well, I should add that only a handful of those I have encountered came to renown in their own time. The vast majority are commonfolk. Still, the cities of Greece at this time in history attract a large number of passers-through; so, when in Greece, I have had the benefit of many meetings. I would speculate this is because that place in my time is, in short, the cradle of arts, culture, and philosophy for all other civilizations yet to emerge in the West.'

After renewing its food supplies at the village through the pass, the army resumed its march. I was finding our plodding along ever more tedious. We were in the land of the Taochi — mountainous, uneven terrain, with only a few trees and scrub. Now in the winter, it was like a rocky moonscape, with the occasional dry skeleton of a thicket. I was always tired, and sometimes cranky.

After four days' march, some of the soldiers must have been growing a little cranky too, as their meals were again becoming less frequent than they would have needed. Food was scarce because the Taochi built their storage sheds within strong fortifications, well away from the roads. A native, taken prisoner at the heights and acting as our guide, explained that these battlements would be difficult to plunder. Should they find one to try in the first place.

On the fifth day of this stretch, after making about ninety miles, a supply fort was spotted at last. Chirisophus had already launched an attack with the light-armoured infantry before Xenophon, with whom Amor and I walked, came on the scene with his hoplites.

Chirisophus greeted us, shouting, 'You have come where you are needed!' He explained that it was vital that they take the position, but he had failed to make any progress with his infantry alone.

It was horrible. A number of his men were lying crushed dead, many others wounded with broken bones. As the soldiers advanced to attack, wagon-loads of stones were rolled down on them.

The worst was yet to come.

Xenophon and Chirisophus again consulted on a strategy, though less formally than the last time. Xenophon's conclusion of it was to banjax the enemy resources — which he said were not limitless — without taking casualties. This meant advancing just so far as the defenders would dump their stones, but from where they could quickly take cover, and avoid being struck.

The first to act on this plan was someone called Callimachus. He positioned himself to advance on the enemy from the shelter of a tree. He would shout and run toward them, down would come tons of rock, at which he nimbly retreated back to safety. Quite a feat, given he was a *mountain* of a man! The Taochi fell for this stunt several times, tipping ten wagons of rock each time, until, as Xenophon predicted, their supplies were exhausted. For the last few ruses, other soldiers got into the act.

Amor explained to me that there was a rivalry between three or four of the Greeks, as to who was bravest, and most resourceful — and who would get to the plunder first! When the stone was finished, they actually fought each other to be the first up the slope, grabbing each other's shields, each pulling the other back.

The fresh shock, however, was that the Taochi then started throwing *women and children* down to their deaths upon them! — and cattle, and then other men! Apparently their custom was that nothing would be taken alive.

One Greek was killed attempting to restrain a man from throwing himself down the gorge, and over they both went.

It was dreadful. But the Ten Thousand prevailed, and left with the fresh food they needed, mainly livestock — oxen, donkeys, and sheep.

Next they marched seven days through the land of the Chalybes, about one hundred and fifty miles. They were fierce and aggressive, the most savage of all the tribes the army had encountered, I was told. Eager to fight, they stalked the Greeks every inch of the way, attacking in close quarters with knives at every opportunity. They wore a thick linen body armour, with a skirt of knotted cords.

When they had picked off an invader, they cut off his head and paraded it in sight of the main column as they marched. Xenophon knew that it was not possible to attack this lot. The best he could do was keep well-fed soldiers, ready to fight, at the flanks — especially at the rear — of his forces, and fight valiantly when attacked.

There were many casualties, and Amor and I were fairly steadily occupied with inspecting the jewelry of the fallen.

It was a relief coming to the river Harpasus, which marked the end of the Chalybes' territory. The river was broad, about four hundred feet, but was not a difficult crossing for the men.

We were now in the land of the Scytheni, a people friendlier to the Greeks. We were getting close to the sea.

Knowing that, I was happy for the soldiers, but unhappy for myself. Arriving at the sea was the end of the march. The end of the line. Margaret — I had decided I would not think of her as Meg, and certainly not as 'mom,' yet — and Arthur would be meeting up with Elizabeth, and then they planned to leave.

Although I knew Amor would comfort and care for me as long as I remained, the thought of being close to the travellers' planned departure made me feel lonely and desperate. They were my best hope to get back to my old life. I'd take a lost mitten for every soldier on this march to be back in the classroom with my little munchkins at Crestwood school now, I thought.

Four days' march from the river, we came to a village where there was food and shelter for the men. We stayed there for three days. While we were there I overheard a conversation between Amor and Arthur, which did little to improve my spirits.

Amor had left me to rest, alongside one of the village shacks. He ambled off around the corner, where, I could hear, he ran into Arthur. Arthur asked him if he had a minute to talk, and Amor said he did.

'The turn of events with Grace and Margaret, and my trip to Canada, have been more complicated that I might have anticipated,' Arthur said.

I think he must have wanted me to overhear — not being able to tell me straight out whatever it was he had on his mind.

'You may have to abandon the idea that the travellers lead straightforward lives, except as you transit time as well as space,' Amor said.

'That is true,' Arthur replied, 'although I will strive to ensure that the present situation is well resolved; and, in doing so, hopefully restore the simplicity we seek to preserve, which you point out.

'The fact is that there are *many* constraints upon us. Large among them being that we cannot slip ahead to see our own future. That is, we cannot travel to any other time where we are "also" present in body. So I cannot, for example, slip ahead to foresee the outcome of Grace's dilemma, as I am also there at the time. This one thing usually *ensures* that the knowledge we gain is of little moment to our own lives. As I once said to Grace, we live them out, happily ignorant about our own personal fortunes ahead.

'I learned something more on my trip, however, that touches on my own future. It may appear to be a comic cosmic loop, like this circumstance with Grace being named after herself, but it is not. It sometimes happens that an incidental idea may arise in, or from, a loop like that; but anything substantive, any original invention, *always* has an original cause or basis.

'I was very fond of Grace's friend Faith, and she me. No romance was advanced, as such, but I promised I would come back to further our friendship. I discussed my plan with Margaret, there in the morrow. When we arrive in England, in 1936, I intend to slip ahead to a time a few weeks after Grace's accident. I will be thirty-three then — so when I arrive in 1962 I will suddenly be twenty-six years younger than Margaret, who lived out the intervening decades.

'Margaret said that was fine with her, as she had enjoyed a happy life over that interim. As well, having become close friends, and seeing the natural bond between her and me, she decided to confide in Faith about our history.'

Amor must have looked a little shocked, as Arthur was silent for a moment.

'There is something further, Amor. I believe that Faith will later have a baby daughter, who in turn has a son. She will keep our secret through her long life — until shortly before her death, when she will tell her fourteen-year-old grandson about the slip device. The boy has a natural brilliance for physics, and later pursues an education as an engineer. Knowing from his grandmother's confidence that such a device is a definite practical possibility, he perseveres in its invention. And succeeds. I believe Faith's grandson is, or was, Gerald, my friend, fallen only months ago fighting for Cyrus. He often spoke of his family, and, while my conclusion *is* only inference, there seems little doubt of the connexion. I had only to hear Faith's full name to know.'

'I now understand the caution you offered me,' Amor said, 'but it was not necessary. These circumstances are related by a simple logic, and are in no way coincidental. The whole strikes me as no more remarkable than any other chain of events in the natural world. Every moment of every day opens to manifold possibilities, and causes and outcomes are necessarily weighted by proximity.'

'Yes, that is true Amor,' I said out loud. But what Arthur said also meant that I may have no bigger purpose to fulfill later. I urgently needed a definite sign that I had a role in the future, some indication that I took some *specific* action, or something — anything at all. But there was less and less, rather than more and more.

And I think somebody somewhere muſt be tolling a bell.

I was more and more tired. Amor had to carry me all the time. There was no sleep to be had over the boundary, but I would lie forward and rest my head on the back of Amor's long, broad neck.

Four days' march from Scytheni, Elizabeth was rejoined with Arthur and Margaret, when the army arrived at the next town. You'd have to call it a city, really. A much larger population than we'd seen up to now, including some Greeks, with many permanent buildings of wood and stone. It was called Gymnias. We were only days from the sea. The fighting should be over for the army now, for this campaign anyway. They still had to pass through some unfriendly territory, but no serious engagement was expected.

Arthur and Margaret had not expected to see Elizabeth until we arrived at Trapezus. She *had* been there, it turned out, disguised as a man, and had become friends with the Greek governor of the territory. When the governor had received news of the tortured army of his countrymen advancing toward safety, Elizabeth suggested to him that she travel to Gymnias, and guide the army through the mountains to the land of the Macrones. Her real intent was to reunite with her friends as early as possible. She did not yet know that the talisman was missing. She had never even seen it! It was given to Gerald as they were all leaving, and then she slipped to a different place.

It was touching, even uplifting, to see their joy at being together again. They embraced each other warmly, and kissed each other's cheeks. Elizabeth was received by other soldiers too, who offered similar greetings. She was instantly the symbol of their deliverance. Her presence embodied the relief of their ordeal coming to an end.

Xenophon was, appropriately, more pragmatic in his thinking, and, while probably not suspicious, received her asking what he — believing she was a man — could promise them. Elizabeth said that within five days she could lead the army to a place where they could see the sea, and volunteered to be put to death if she failed.

'Something of a formality,' Amor assured me.

And the army proceeded on its march. Because Elizabeth was the centre of attention for a time, I was not introduced to her straight away. We did not have the opportunity to speak for two days.

She played her role convincingly. For example, when we crossed into enemy territory, she instructed Xenophon to torch the land, the same as Napoleon did marching into Russia.

This hostility improved Xenophon's confidence in her. He preferred that she would be guiding his army out of loathing for the enemy, rather than as a generosity to the Greeks. For him, and for the whole army, that made her more trustworthy. It was a brilliant insight on Elizabeth's part.

There came a time, on the second day past Gymnias, that Arthur saw an opportunity to introduce us. He was with Margaret, and Elizabeth — always under scrutiny — was pretending to be giving them instructions.

They were marching in the forward column with Xenophon, who had taken the lead for the day, having put someone called Eurylochus in charge of the hoplites in the rear. Since Gymnias, Amor and I had been following a short way behind the travellers.

Then, as we walked along, Arthur gave Amor a little signal to come forward to where they were.

'Amor and Grace, I am very happy that you should know our close friend Elizabeth.'

Although Amor and I had been watching the three of them for two days, it was like I was seeing her for the first time — or, rather, *looking* at her for the first time. Her face beamed. As our eyes met I felt a fresh lightness inside, a renewed energy. It was spooky! She was divinely beautiful — I could hardly believe she could pass for a man! — a dark complexion colouring the finest of features.

'I am very glad to know you, Grace. I am fully informed of your dilemma, and pledge my assiduous effort to help you.'

Then Amor said something very strange.

'I believe you know me, Rhiannon,' he said.

'Yes I do,' she said.

They went on their way then, back to their duties on the march. I did not ask Amor why he called her by that name. There seemed to be something very personal about it, a confidence between them. I had the feeling that even if he explained I would not understand, so I let it go.

On the third day, walking by herself, Elizabeth suddenly turned and waved to Amor to come up alongside.

'Grace,' she said, 'I understand you have an interest in our meeting with Job.'

'Yes, I do!' I replied.

'Arthur wished that I tell you of it, because, while we were there, I was the only one who could hear the voice of The Tempest.'

'The Tempest?' I said.

'The Creator,' Amor said softly.

'We came to the place after Job had suffered his misfortunes, as his friends sat with him in silence. The Tempest tolerated, or ignored, our presence there, as he ignored the presence of insects and birds — though, I believe, he volunteered a supply of food that was made available to us. We stayed far enough away that we could not be detected by Job and his friends, but close enough that we could hear the voice. That *I* could hear the voice. While deaf to him, Arthur and Margaret felt the wind, and the trembling ground. His very presence was dramatic.'

'So he really *was* there?' I said, feeling ignorant.

'Oh yes,' Elizabeth said, 'but be clear on one thing. The Tempest is The Creator. He spoke to Job in the form, or person, of the God he had created. The Tempest created all things, including God, including Satan, including Valhalla, the light, the dark, the earth, the heavens, including good, and including evil.'

Elizabeth spoke with gripping warmth and authority.

'Before the time of Job, The Tempest had a relationship with humankind. Perhaps because it was his work, and because he is vast beyond the whole universe, he did not *treat* his creation with the considerate regard which his people expected. The Tempest, known to his chosen as their Lord God — an original concept he changed and developed as time went on — became *alienated* from his people. Or rather, his people became alienated from him, finding him to be alternately cruel, punishing, and neglectful. They fashioned a new likeness of this God for themselves — a *reliable* God, as Xenophon has been a *reliable* friend and leader to his men on this march — into books of laws. While these were genuinely intended as devotions to The Tempest, they were in fact the final estrangement from him.'

Elizabeth looked at me softly, giving me a minute to take that in.

'The dialogue with Job was the last time The Tempest spoke with man. When a friendship has soured, one tends to lash out at the estranged companion. The Tempest, the estranged father, there had a last lashing out at his unhappy sons and daughters.

'While I am reluctant to make any comparison with human feelings, it was as though he had been hurt — which Job's submissiveness only made worse, like a second insult. You see, when someone, even The Tempest, has been hurt, they want *healing*, not *justice*. Job's devotion was justice. He was not *capable* of healing. It may be that The Tempest himself recognized this — as though he were lonely for a worthy companion, but recognized then he could not create an equal to himself. His ways and workings, his creation, were utterly magnificent, and utterly intricate. None of his created could be, by nature, as profoundly intricate as the whole creation.

'We didn't approach Job until a few days after the dialogue was over. The Tempest had begun restoring his estate. I told him who and what we were, and he seemed to believe me. I suppose having just had the experience he did, our story did not seem far-fetched. As well, we *knew* what had transpired, which was for him an immediate bond. We talked mostly about the voice.

'We did not stay any length of time past that. We had learned what we came there to know. When we told the old man we were leaving, he gave Gerald the ring, recalling what we had discussed about the voice, saying, *This is the bridge.*'

'Yes, I have heard that,' I said, 'but why did he give *Gerald* the object, when *you* experienced the voice?'

'Because I am a woman,' she replied. 'This is the custom of his people.'

She scrunched her lips between her thumb and forefinger. 'One more thing, Grace. The Tempest may be alienated from this world, but his complex invention carries on under its own divine momentum, and it is a great and wondrous thing. It has no objective value, however — you *give* it value by the power of your personality. This is one of the lessons of Job. But what finer reward could there be than, for example, the love of friends?'

Then it happened. On the fifth day past Gymnias. The rear guard had been pestered by bandits the day before, whom they turned around and ambushed, killing or capturing a number of them. The Greeks' determination never waned.

Now shouts were heard. The rear guard, including Xenophon (who had resumed his usual post), thought the head of the column must be under attack on the mountain, Thekes, ahead.

The shouts got louder and louder, and we could see in the distance waves of men running forward, as they respectively got closer to the ruckus.

Xenophon was visibly alarmed, but acted with cool efficiency, as he usually did. He called for a horse for himself, and ordered one of his generals, Lycus, to mobilize the cavalry. This cavalry had only been formed in Gymnias, where Xenophon had been given some horses, but had been put to work at the rear of the procession straight away, dealing with the native bandits.

They rode off as hard as they could — Amor and I following close behind — in full battle ready, to assist at the front.

Xenophon had ordered the hoplites to prepare to fight, and to follow up at full speed. They were instantly dressed and ready, and the *chunk, chunk, chunk* of their heavy-armoured quick march filled the air behind us.

Then we heard it. Xenophon heard it too. He stiffened on his mount at first — but then his face softened, even seemed to blanch a little.

'The sea! The sea!' they were calling. 'The sea! The sea!'

Xenophon wept openly at the sight, as did his generals and captains. There was hardly a dry eye on the hill, in fact, and they all embraced each other. There was no rowdiness, however. This was sober bedrock-of-the-soul relief, and they all felt it.

They built a monument at the top of the rise. It was made of stone, together with some staves and ox-hide shields they had taken from the native bandits.

Elizabeth took part in its construction, slashing the captured shields into pieces, as a true enemy would, and encouraging others to do so. One of the generals shouted out that this guide had been their deliverer, and Elizabeth was suddenly the focus of a tremendous celebration!

Xenophon himself came forward with the gift of a horse, another officer with a fine silver cup, someone else with a beautiful robe, and another with gold coins.

'What I want for your gratitude, my friends, is your rings!' she said in a loud voice.

And she was showered — a rain of gold bands. There must have been fifty at her feet, with much cheering and laughter. Two of the captains helped her pick them up into a skin bag.

'Amor!' she called, 'Arthur! Grace! Margaret! I think I have it.'

Elizabeth then spoke to Xenophon, directing him to a village down the other side of the mountain where the army could camp, and carefully pointing out the road which led through the country of the Macrones, to Trapezus. It was evening by that time, and she told him she would be leaving that night.

I was tense with fear and apprehension.

Arthur and Margaret did not stay with the army, but rather met Elizabeth at a secluded spot round the other side of the hill. Amor and I joined them there. On top of my anxiety, I could hardly budge for fatigue. I seemed to be drifting in and out. Only the music remained steady in my mind. 'Thank you,' I was saying. 'Thank you.' I knew the song was a thing apart from the singer, especially here, but it had still been like a friend to me. *There's nothing left here inside of me.* I was holding onto Amor for dear life.

'We have the ring, but still do not know its use or meaning,' Margaret said. 'All I can think is it cannot be magic — or at least that would seem very unlikely for that devoted old Hebrew.'

'What is written on the ring?' Amor asked.

'Just three letters,' Arthur said, 'right to left, *shin – yud – resh*, 'שׁיר.' A common *shoresh*.'

'Yes, a root, if that's a clue,' Elizabeth said. 'The word is *shir* — which as a noun means a song or poem, or alone as a verb, the imperative *sing*.'

'Sing?' Amor said. 'Sing.'

Then he came to life underneath me like never before.

'Sing. Sing. SING! *Sing!* Grace! *Sing! Sing!*'

'Sing? What do you mean, "sing"?' I asked.

'Sing! Sing with the music,' Amor said, 'that is how you direct your spirit back. The MUSIC.'

'I can't sing,' I said, embarrassed even in my distress.

'Listen to the music, and *sing!* Grace, *please,*' Amor pleaded.

I could hear the music, the tune and harmonies, but I could not understand the lyrics, except the chorus. So I just sang the chorus over and over again.

Gimme the future, gimme the future, gimme the future, gimme the future with a modern girl.

I really began to *feel* the rhythm, and sang louder and harder, over and over again.

Gimme the future, gimme the future, gimme the future, gimme the future with a modern girl. Gimme the future, gimme the future . . . .

I was holding tightly to Amor, and it was like . . . it was like we began to fly together, soaring through space, and at terrific speed.

I'm back, I thought. I knew I was back.

I opened my eyes, and there in the room was Margaret — that is, *Mom!* — and Faith. And Elizabeth!

'You will be well,' I heard someone say. It was Amor.

Epilogue

Our lives are not forever. *As the Goddess Night nurses the babe Sleep to one breast, and the babe Death to the other*, I once said to Grace. Her natural life ended with illness thirty-nine years following that last eve on Thekes. She was wed to a good man, and bore two fine children, a boy and a girl. She fulfilled her ambitions in education, and with other compassionate causes. With her husband, she enjoyed material well-being, while the earth could still provide it. Most precious of all, she and I knew a rare friendship. When she was gone, I returned to my home, where we had first met, and resumed pacing the centuries, till I may also expire.